Ultimate BUSINESS PLANNING

For Visionary Start-Ups & Revolutionary Companies

Written by
Norman David Roussell, MBA

Published by

START SMART

ISBN-13: 978-0979620140
ISBN-10: 0979620147

Ultimate **BUSINESS PLANNING**

For Visionary Start-Ups & Revolutionary Companies

Table of Contents

Ultimate BUSINESS PLANNING

For Visionary Start-Ups & Revolutionary Companies

Table of Contents
(Continued)

APPENDIX: *MWI Widgets, Inc.- Sample Business Plan*

Faith. Perseverance. Fortitude.
"I am an entrepreneur!"

Ultimate BUSINESS PLANNING
For Visionary Start-Ups & Revolutionary Companies

Ultimate Business Planning for Visionary Start-Ups & Revolutionary Companies (Ultimate Planning) is an information-gathering workbook to help you write the ultimate business plan. This workbook is a companion to *Ultimate Strategy: The Art & Science of Strategic Business Planning for Innovative Start-Ups & Emerging Businesses (Ultimate Strategy)*. When used together, the workbooks provide the step-by-step guidance you need to develop a comprehensive strategic plan and write the ultimate bank, management or investor-ready business plan.

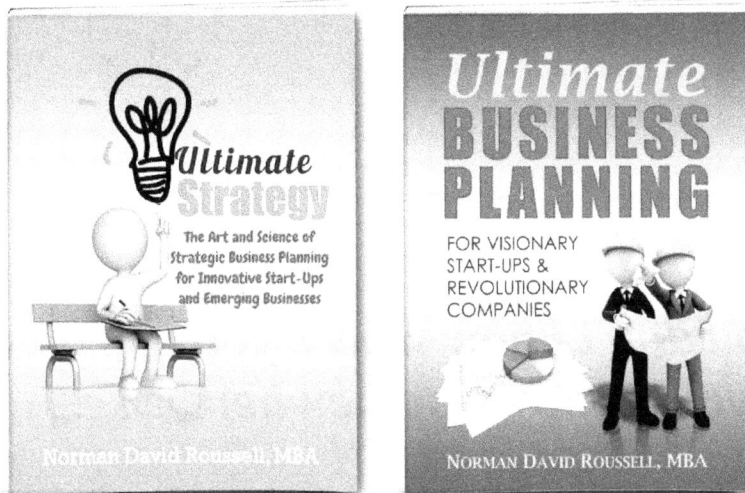

Ultimate Business Planning Tips
✓ Read the entire workbook before you begin to write your ultimate business plan;
✓ Perform an internet search or visit your local library to get more information on any topic you need additional guidance; and
✓ Consult a professional if necessary to complete your ultimate business plan.

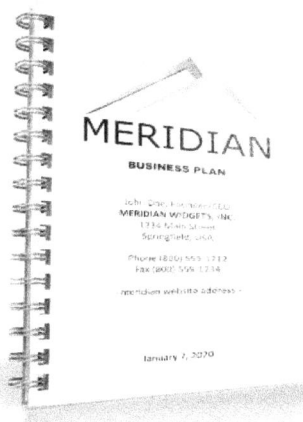

Sample Business Plan
The example text, tables, charts and financials that appear throughout this workbook are based on the fictitious company, *Meridian Widgets, Inc.*, (MWI).

A completed business plan for MWI, using the examples that appear throughout this workbook, appears in the appendix at the end of this workbook.

"If you don't know where you are going,
you'll end up somewhere else."

Yogi Berra

Ultimate BUSINESS PLANNING
For Visionary Start-Ups & Revolutionary Companies

WHAT IS A BUSINESS PLAN?

A business plan is a document that summarizes the operational, marketing, sales and financial objectives of a business to show how the business will grow and succeed over time.

The ultimate business plan is...

✓ The transformation of your dreams of entrepreneurial success into their monetary equivalent;

✓ One of the tools that will help you raise start-up or expansion capital for your business; and

✓ The cornerstone of every successful business.

The ultimate business plan should answer the who, what, when, where, how, and why about your business. For example,

- Who will manage your business?
- What is your business model?
- When will you open for business?
- Where will you sell your **products and services**?
- How will you market your products and services?
- Why are you seeking capital?

> *Products and services* is used throughout this workbook to also refer to a single product and/or a single service.

WHO NEEDS A BUSINESS PLAN?

Banks need a business plan to determine if a business will generate enough cash flow to meet a monthly repayment obligation if approved for a loan.

Most, if not all, banks will require a business plan to accompany a business loan request. Asking for a business plan is a banker's way of eliminating those entrepreneurs who are not prepared to start or grow a successful business.

Bankers assume that if you are not willing to put in the time and effort to research and write a business plan, you are not likely to put forth the effort to ensure a loan is repaid. This may or may not be a true assumption, but it exists and it is a major reason banks require a business plan.

3

Ultimate BUSINESS PLANNING
For Visionary Start-Ups & Revolutionary Companies

Business owners need a business plan to gain buy-in- agreement with a plan or idea- on the mission, vision, objectives and strategies the business.

A business plan is to business owners what blueprints are to construction contractors- a roadmap to success. A business plan provides business owners a roadmap that helps them stay on track with their business plans.

A business plan also helps business owners compare planned results to actual results. By comparing planned results to actual results, business owners can implement the changes required to build a more efficient and more profitable company.

Table 1 is an example of how planned results can differ from actual results. As a result of actual sales, the business owners may want to commit more resources to marketing Industrial Widgets and Deluxe Widgets, or develop a new marketing campaign to increase sales of its Standard Widgets.

Table 1: Comparison of planned to actual results

Product	PLANNED Units Sold	ACTUAL Units Sold	Difference
Industrial Widgets	500	600	+100
Deluxe Widgets	1,000	1,300	+300
Standard Widgets	2,000	1,800	-200
Total	**3,500**	**3,700**	**+200**

Investors need a business plan to determine if a business can be successful, competitive and a good investment.

Like bankers, investors use a business plan as a gatekeeping mechanism to "weed out" those entrepreneurs who are not serious, or even worse, prepared.

Even when the investors are your friends and family, a business plan goes a long way in proving to them that your business idea is viable, your business model is sound and your business will be a good investment.

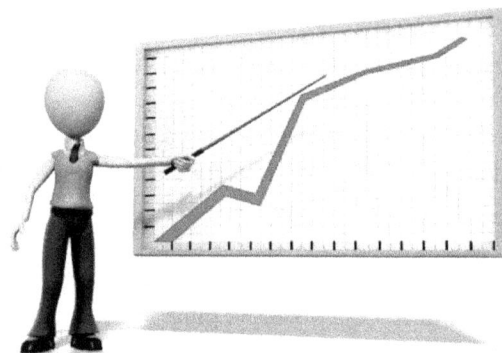

Ultimate BUSINESS PLANNING

For Visionary Start-Ups & Revolutionary Companies

TWENTY QUESTIONS

Before you begin to write your ultimate business plan, you should know the answers to the following questions about starting, managing, marketing and growing your business. Use the worksheets on pages 6-8 to answer the questions below. If you do not know an answer yet, come back to the question later. If a question does not apply to your business (For example, if you provide a service but do not manufacture a product) answer "Not Applicable" or "N/A".

1. What products and services will you manufacture, distribute or sell to customers?

2. What licenses, certifications and training do you need to operate your business?

3. What is the purpose of your products and services?

4. Who will manage your business?

5. Who will work in the business on a day-to-day basis?

6. Who are your major competitors?

7. Who are your potential customers?

8. What is your target market?

9. How you will bring your products and services to market?

10. What are the trends in the industry?

11. How will you set your prices or fees?

12. Why will customers buy your products and services versus the competition?

13. What are your sales objectives for the first 12-months?

14. How much money do you need to start or expand your business?

15. From where or whom will you get the money to start or expand your business?

16. How will you generate revenue and manage expenses to ensure you earn a profit?

17. Where do you want your company to be in one year, three years and five years?

18. What type of computers and software do you need to manage sales, clients, inventory, etc.?

19. What types of insurance do you need to protect your business and personal assets?

20. Who will manage accounting, payroll, taxes, human resources, etc., for your business?

Ultimate BUSINESS PLANNING
For Visionary Start-Ups & Revolutionary Companies

Twenty Questions

1. What products and services will you manufacture, distribute or sell to customers?

2. What licenses, certifications and training do you need to operate your business?

3. What is the purpose of your products and services?

4. Who will manage your business?

5. Who will work in the business on a day-to-day basis?

6. Who are your major competitors?

7. Who are your potential customers?

Ultimate **BUSINESS PLANNING**

For Visionary Start-Ups & Revolutionary Companies

Twenty Questions (continued)

8. What is your target market?

9. How you will bring your products and services to market?

10. What are the trends in the industry?

11. How will you set your prices or fees?

12. Why will customers buy your products and services versus the competition?

13. What are your sales objectives for the first 12-months?

14. How much money do you need to start or expand your business?

Twenty Questions (continued)

15. From where or whom will you get the money to start or expand your business?

16. How will you generate revenue and manage expenses to ensure you earn a profit?

17. Where do you want your company to be in one year, three years and five years?

18. What type of computers and software do you need to manage sales, clients, inventory, etc.?

19. What types of insurance do you need to protect your business and personal assets?

20. Who will manage accounting, payroll, taxes, human resources, etc., for your business?

RESEARCHING YOUR ULTIMATE BUSINESS PLAN

It is important to research your business idea, business model and the market for your products and services before, not after, you write your ultimate business plan. If you have written a one-page strategic business plan, as recommended, you have already refined your business idea and developed a business model that creates, delivers and captures value for your customers and you have already defined your company's mission, vision, values, objectives and strategies.

For additional help researching your ultimate business plan, visit the websites below. In addition to online workshops and tools, your local SBA and Score offices may be able to provide you with one-on-one management and technical assistance to help you start and grow your business and write your ultimate business plan.

Website	Provides
www.sba.gov	The U.S. Small Business Administration (SBA) aids, counsels, assists and protects the interests of small business concerns through entrepreneurial development, access to capital, government contracting and advocacy.
www.score.org	SCORE is a non-profit organization with over 13,000 volunteers who provide confidential business counseling to entrepreneurs at no charge.
www.census.gov	Census.gov provides up-to-date statistical data on the U.S. population, U.S. business and industry and the U.S. economy.
www.business.usa.gov	Business USA is a one-stop-shop to make it easier for businesses to access services to help them grow.
www.hoovers.com	Hoovers provides in-depth research and information on U.S. and global companies and industries.
www.forrester.com	Forrester analyzes trends in technology and how they impact businesses.
www.bplans.com	BPlans.com provides free sample business plans, business planning software, business planning calculators and other business planning resources.

Go to *Small Business Resources for Success,* beginning on page 133, for a comprehensive list of over 30 agencies, organizations and websites to help you start, manage and grow your business.

Tip! Visit the websites of the leading companies in your industry to gain insight on how successful companies describe their business, products and services.

"If your dreams don't scare you,
they aren't big enough."
Muhammad Ali

FACTORS THAT INFLUENCE BANKERS AND INVESTORS

In addition to conducting your research, you should understand the major factors that banks and investors consider when evaluating a business plan. Those factors, known as the "7Cs", include:

Credit

Banks, and most investors, evaluate the borrowing and repayment history of a business owner by reviewing personal credit reports and scores (FICO® scores) and business credit reports and scores (Paydex® scores).

A FICO® score of 720 or above and a Paydex® score of 80 or above indicates that you and your business are creditworthy.

Visit **www.myfico.com** to learn more about personal credit scores and read *Principles of Building Business Credit* (Amazon.com) to learn how to build business credit in as little as 120-days.

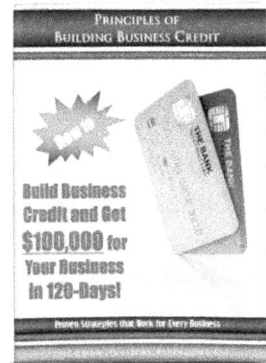

Capital

If your business is a start-up, you should have a meaningful amount of personal capital to invest in its success. For example, if you are applying for a $100,000.00 loan, a bank may want you, as the business owner, to have $10,000.00, $20,000.00 or more in cash available to invest in the business.

Unfortunately for most entrepreneurs, sweat equity usually cannot replace cash or other tangible assets as your capital contribution to secure a loan.

Collateral

Most banks, and some investors, will require that you pledge personal or business assets, such as land or equipment, to ensure they can recoup the balance of a loan or investment in the event your business fails. If you are borrowing from friends and family, showing that you have collateral that can be liquidated if the venture fails can help "seal the deal".

Conditions

Whether you are competing in a local, regional, national or global marketplace, you should know the economic, political, environmental and social conditions affecting your business and industry. You should be prepared to explain to bankers, investors and other stakeholders how your company will succeed under those conditions.

Capacity

Capacity refers to your management experience, qualifications and financial ability to repay a loan or investment. For example, a company with four employees may have the management capacity, in years of experience, to oversee a $15 million-dollar project, but may not have the size capacity, in number of employees, to ensure the job is completed on schedule and on budget.

Character

The moral and ethical qualities of a business owner, character, play a vital role in securing start-up or expansion capital, winning new clients and increasing sales.

In other words, good character counts and it is critical to your long-term success in business.

Cash Flow

Cash flow- money that comes in and goes out of a business during a day, week, month, quarter or year- is an indicator of whether your business will generate enough revenue to cover monthly operational expenses and a monthly bank loan or investor repayment obligation.

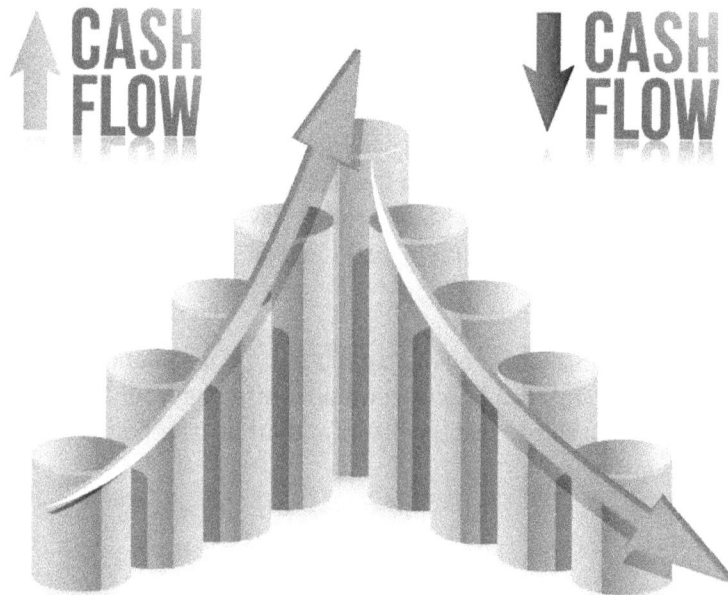

Ultimate BUSINESS PLANNING
For Visionary Start-Ups & Revolutionary Companies

GROWTH STRATEGIES 101

Most companies want to grow over time and there are several ways to do it. Understanding how businesses grow helps you better plan and write your ultimate business plan. Review the growth strategies below and apply one or more of those strategies to your long-term business growth plans.

INTENSIVE GROWTH STRATEGIES

Market Penetration	Market Development	Alternative Channels	Product Development
Sell more current products and services to existing customers.	Sell more current products and services to new customers and/or new markets.	Sell current products and services in different ways.	Develop new products and services to sell to existing and new customers.
♦	♦	♦	♦
Example: *Sell 20,000 more MWI widgets to existing customers.*	*Example:* *Expand MWI widget sales to South America and Europe.*	*Example:* *Sell MWI widgets online.*	*Example:* *MWI's new X-Widget.*

INTEGRATIVE GROWTH STRATEGIES

Horizontal	Backward	Forward
Buy a competing business or businesses.	Buying one or more suppliers as a way to control the company's supply chain and lower costs.	Buying companies within the company's distribution channel.
♦	♦	♦
Example: *Purchase ACME Widgets to increase capacity.*	*Example:* *Buy an aluminum supplier to decrease costs.*	*Example:* *Buy Widget Depo stores to ensure MWI widgets have retail outlets.*

DIVERSIFICATION GROWTH STRATEGY

Growing the company by purchasing unrelated companies or product lines.

♦

Example: Purchase a chain of fast food restaurants to diversify MWI's revenue sources.

Ultimate BUSINESS PLANNING

For Visionary Start-Ups & Revolutionary Companies

Notes and Worksheet Page

Ultimate BUSINESS PLANNING
For Visionary Start-Ups & Revolutionary Companies

COMPONENTS OF THE ULTIMATE BUSINESS PLAN

Executive Summary
SECTION 1 OF THE ULTIMATE BUSINESS PLAN

The business plan begins with the executive summary. The executive summary is a one- or two-page synopsis of the entire plan. The goal of the executive summary is to answer critical questions about the business, while enticing the reader to review the entire plan. Although the executive summary is at the beginning of the plan, it is usually written last since it is a summary of the entire plan.

The executive summary should include, at a minimum, the following information:

- A brief description of the company and its ownership
- A description of your products and services
- Mission Statement
- Vision Statement
- Values Statement
- Objectives
- Start-Up or Expansion Costs Table
- **Pro Forma** Sales Graph
- Keys to Success

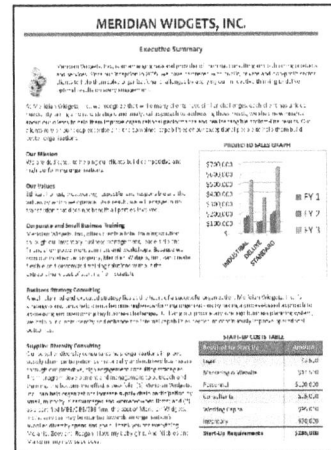

Pro Forma (def.)
Projected, assumed or forecasted.

The executive summary is both a component of your business plan and a stand-alone document you can give to bankers, potential investors and other stakeholders to gain buy-in about your plans.

Management Plan
SECTION 2 OF THE ULTIMATE BUSINESS PLAN

The management plan is where you provide information about the company, the owners and staff and discuss how your team's experience will help you manage and grow the business.

The management plan should include, at a minimum, the following information:

- An in-depth description of the company and its products and services
- Owners, their ownership percentages, experience and duties
- Key personnel and their roles
- Personnel Plan and Table
- Employee Benefit Plans
- SWOT Analysis
- Milestones
- Exit Strategy

Include an organizational chart along with résumés of owners, key personnel and consultants in the supporting documents section of your business plan.

Products and Services
SECTION 3 OF THE ULTIMATE BUSINESS PLAN

A business is not a business without products to sell or services to provide. In this section, describe your products and services and discuss why people will buy them from your company.

Products and services should include, at a minimum, the following information:

- A description of your products and services
- The purpose of your products and services
- **Features** and **benefits** of your products and services
- Patents, trademarks and copyrights
- Licensing and franchise agreements
- Your company's future products and services

Features and Benefits
(Page 59)

Marketing Plan
SECTION 4 OF THE ULTIMATE BUSINESS PLAN

What good is a multi-million-dollar product or service if you do not know how to get it to your customers?

Your marketing plan encompasses all the activities it takes to get a product or service in the hands of consumers. Marketing is so critical to the overall success of the business that you may need to write a separate, more comprehensive marketing plan in addition to writing your ultimate business plan.

The marketing plan should include, at a minimum, the following information:

- Market Summary
- Market Segmentation Analysis
- Target Market Analysis
- Market Trend Analysis
- Marketing Strategy

"4Ps" Marketing Mix
Product • Price • Promotion • Place

(Page 65)

Website and Social Media Plans
SECTION 5 OF THE ULTIMATE BUSINESS PLAN

Your website and social media plans explain how you will inform, attract and engage clients through the internet and other digital communication formats. Your website and social media plans can help you leverage limited marketing dollars to make your start-up or growing business appear as large as a multi-national corporation.

Your website should have e-mail capabilities (For example, John@MWIWidgets.com) and should, at a minimum, include:

- Information about the company
- Information about your products and services
- A way for potential clients to contact your company

Many websites also include:

- Articles written by experts within your company
- Affiliate links and ads
- A downloadable brochure and other content
- A calendar of events
- Pictures and videos of your products and services
- Client testimonials
- A newsletter or blog

Social media helps your company interact with clients and potential clients, it keeps your clients informed of trends in the marketplace and it helps generate buzz, leads and new clients for your business. Your social media plan describes how you will utilize social media platforms like Facebook, Twitter and Instagram to build your company's brand awareness.

For example, your social media plan may include:

- Daily Twitter posts
- Daily blog posts
- Weekly Facebook posts
- Monthly YouTube Video posts
- **RSS feeds** to and from your website

Rich Site Summary (RSS) Feeds (def.)
RSS feeds are a family of web feed formats used to frequently update internet content in a standardized format.

"5Cs" of Social Media Marketing
Content • Conversations • Community
Connections • Consistency

(Page 81)

Ultimate BUSINESS PLANNING
For Visionary Start-Ups & Revolutionary Companies

Sales Plan
SECTION 6 OF THE ULTIMATE BUSINESS PLAN

Your sales plan is where you identify the number of units, **Table 2**, of your products and services you plan to sell each month, quarter and **fiscal year** (FY). Your sales plan also shows the revenue generated from each product or service, **Table 3**, and the total revenue generated each year.

Table 2: Sample product sales table by units for FYs 1-3

Product	Unit Sales FY-1	Unit Sales FY-2	Unit Sales FY-3	Total
Industrial Widgets	100,000	125,000 (+25%)	156,250 (+25%)	381,250
Deluxe Widgets	200,000	240,000 (+20%)	288,000 (+20%)	728,000
Standard Widgets	250,000	325,000 (+30%)	422,500 (+30%)	997,500
X-Widgets	----	----	32,500 (New)	32,500
Total	**550,000**	**690,000 (≈25%)**	**900,000**	**2,140,000**

Table 3: Sample product sales table by product revenue FYs 1-3

Product	Selling Price	Revenue FY-1	Revenue FY-2	Revenue FY-3	Total Revenue FYs 1-3
Industrial Widgets	$8.50	$850,000	$1,062,500	$1,328,125	$3,240,625
Deluxe Widgets	$3.50	$700,000	$840,000	$1,008,000	$2,548,000
Standard Widgets	$1.80	$450,000	$585,000	$760,500	$1,795,000
X-Widgets	$59.25	$0	$0	$1,925,625	$1,925,625
Total		**$2,000,000**	**$2,487,500**	**$5,022,250**	**$9,509,750**

Your sales plan should include, at a minimum, the following information:

- Sales plan summary
- Sales plan table by units
- Sales plan revenue table

Tip! *If you do not have a set price for a product or service, you can use the average revenue per sale method to determine a selling price. For example, if you charge fees ranging from $50.00 to $100.00 for a service, you can assume the average revenue per sale is $75.00 [($50.00+$100.00) ÷ 2]. Multiply $75.00 by the number of services (For example, clients or units) you expect to provide or sell to determine annual sales.*

Financial Plan
SECTION 7 OF THE ULTIMATE BUSINESS PLAN

Your financial plan provides the numerical details about what your business is projected to earn and spend during its first three years of operation. You can have a great management team, new and innovative products and services and a marketing plan that shows that you reach customers, but without financials that make sense, the business plan is worthless.

Your financial plan will include, at a minimum, the following information:

- Financial Plan Summary
- Start-Up or Expansion Cost Summary and Table (From Section 1: Executive Summary)
- Break-Even Point Analysis
- Sales Forecast Table (From Section 6: Sales Plan)
- Pro Forma Profit and Loss Statement
- Pro Forma Cash Flow Statement
- Pro Forma Balance Sheet
- Ratio Analysis

Other Key Elements of Your Business Plan

SWOT Analysis
INCLUDED IN THE MANAGEMENT PLAN
Discussed in detail beginning on page 51.

Milestones
INCLUDED IN THE MANAGEMENT PLAN
Discussed in detail on page 55.

Exit Strategy
INCLUDED IN THE MANAGEMENT PLAN
Discussed in detail on page 57.

Supporting Documents

INCLUDED IN THE APPENDIX OF YOUR BUSINESS PLAN

Bankers and investors usually require supporting documents with a business plan to make a final decision about a loan or investment. A comprehensive list of supporting documents appears on page 121 of this workbook.

Some of the supporting documents you typically need include:

Tip! Never, ever submit a document to a banker or investor that is not required or has not been requested. Never!

Ultimate BUSINESS PLANNING
For Visionary Start-Ups & Revolutionary Companies

FORMAT OF THE ULTIMATE BUSINESS PLAN

The following is the recommended format for your ultimate business plan. Remember, every section listed below may not apply to your business. Omit any sections or topics that do not apply to your business. Conversely, add any section or topic, not included below, that may be required for your industry or by a bank or investor.

1.0. Executive Summary
1.1. Company Background Summary
1.2. Products and Services Summary
1.3. Mission Statement
1.4. Vision Statement
1.5. Values Statement
1.6. Objectives
1.7. Start-Up Costs Summary and Table
1.8. Pro Forma Sales Graph
1.9. Keys to Success

2.0. Management Plan
2.1. Management Plan Summary
2.1.1. Company Ownership
2.1.2. Key Personnel
2.1.3. Board of Directors or Managers
2.1.4. Consultants (Master Mind Group)
2.2. Personnel Plan and Table
2.3. Employee Benefit Plans
2.4. SWOT Analysis
2.5. Milestones
2.6. Exit Strategy

3.0. Products and Services
3.1. Products and Services Summary
3.2. Features and Benefits of the Products and Services
3.3. Patents, Trademarks and Copyrights
3.4. Licensing and Franchise Agreements
3.5. Future Products and Services

4.0. Marketing Plan
4.1. Market Analysis Summary
4.2. Market Segmentation Analysis
4.3. Target Market Analysis
4.4. Market Trend Analysis
4.5. Marketing Strategy

5.0. Website and Social Media Plans
    5.1. Website Development Plan
    5.2. Social Media Development Plan

6.0. Sales Plan
    6.1. Sales Plan Summary
    6.2. Sales Plan Table (Units)
    6.2. Sales Plan Table (Revenue)

7.0. Financial Plan
    7.1. Financial Plan Summary
    7.2. Start-Up (Expansion) Cost Summary and Table
    7.3. Break-Even Point Analysis
    7.4. Pro Forma Sales Forecast
    7.5. Pro Forma Income Statement
    7.6. Pro Forma Cash Flow Statement
    7.7. Pro Forma Balance Sheet
    7.8. Ratio Analysis

Appendix
    Supporting Documents

"Your business plan may have more or fewer sections, depending on the level of detail required by bankers, investors or owners."

FRONT MATTER

Cover Page

The cover page includes the name, logo, address, phone number, fax number and website of the company, along with the name of the owners and the date the plan was prepared.

Sample Cover Page

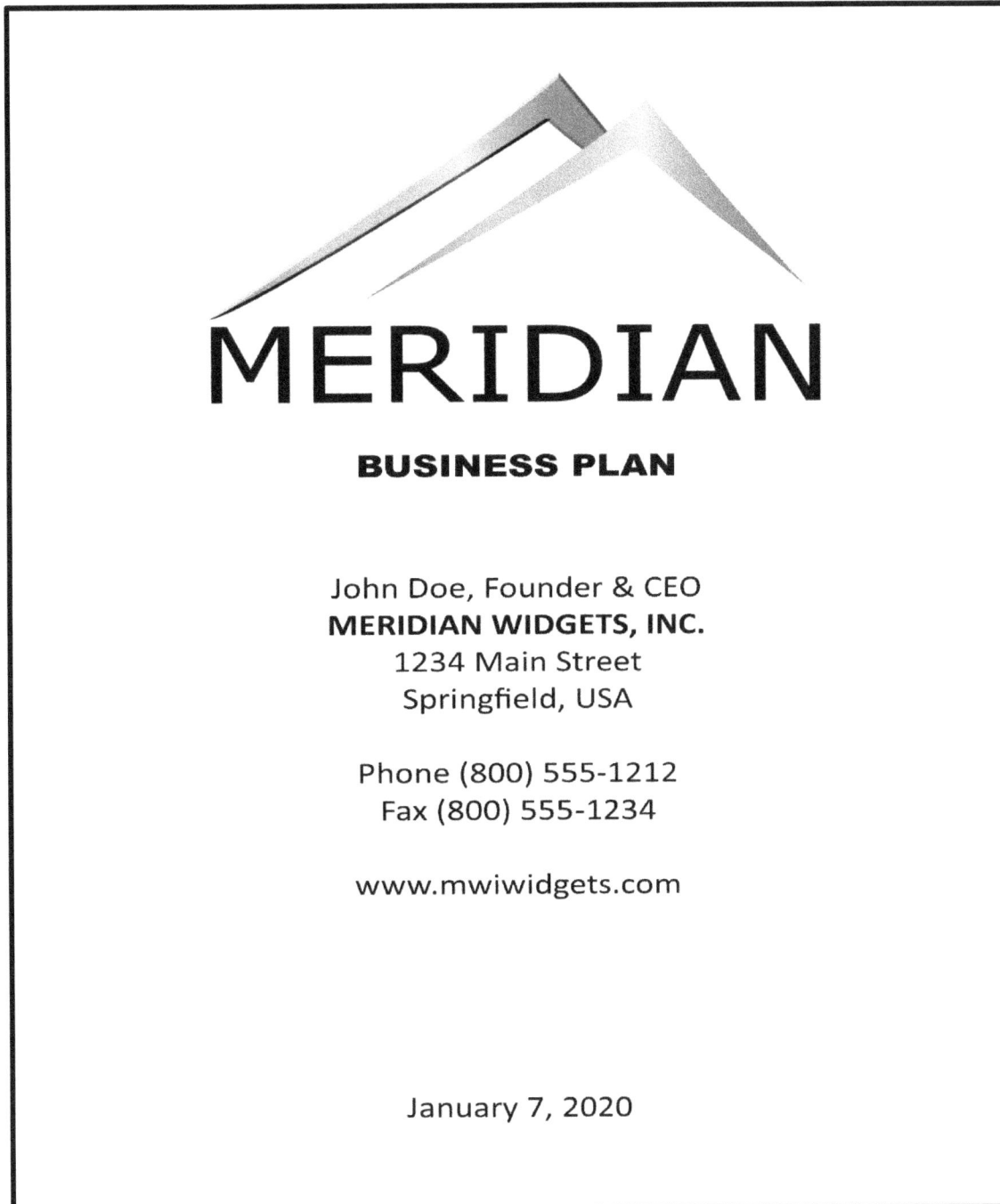

MERIDIAN

BUSINESS PLAN

John Doe, Founder & CEO
MERIDIAN WIDGETS, INC.
1234 Main Street
Springfield, USA

Phone (800) 555-1212
Fax (800) 555-1234

www.mwiwidgets.com

January 7, 2020

Cover Letter

In a short letter, thank the reader in advance for reviewing your business plan and inform him or her that you are available to discuss the plan in detail. If your plan includes a loan proposal, state the amount requested and how you will use and repay the loan.

Sample Cover Letter

MERIDIAN

January 7, 2020

Dear Reader:

Thank you for taking time to review our company's business plan. I believe that you will see the great potential that we have in building a successful widget manufacturing and distribution company over the next three (3) years.

My company is seeking a $100,000 loan to purchasing state-of-the-industry widget manufacturing equipment. With the equipment we will produce our new X-Widget, which will help MWI double revenues within three years. The increased capacity and new product will generate more than enough revenue and cash flow to repay the loan.

If you have any questions about our company or our business plan that you would like to discuss in person, I am available to meet at your convenience.

Again, thank you in advance for reviewing our business plan.

Sincerely yours,

John Doe

John Doe, Founder & CEO

Confidentiality Agreement

The confidentiality agreement is designed to prevent readers from discussing or disseminating your business plan without your written permission. Number each copy of your business plan that you distribute and have every recipient sign two copies of the confidentiality agreement. Retain one copy of the confidentiality agreement for your records.

Sample Confidentiality Agreement

MERIDIAN

CONFIDENTIALITY AGREEMENT

The reader of this business plan acknowledges that the information contained herein is personal and confidential and cannot be discussed, copied or disseminated without the prior written consent of the owner of Meridian Widgets, Inc., Mr. John Doe.

Business Plan Copy 1 of 10 delivered to Mr. John Q. Banker on 01/07/2020.

Acknowledgement of receipt by

John Q. Banker

John Q. Banker

Ultimate BUSINESS PLANNING
For Visionary Start-Ups & Revolutionary Companies

Table of Contents

List each section, identified on pages 19 and 20, with its corresponding page number. Separate each supporting document with a numbered tab divider and list each document in the table of contents.

Include every section and sub-section →

TIP! *The length of your business plan will depend on the complexity of the business and the type of financing you are seeking. A standard business plan should be no less than 12 pages and no more than 25 pages, excluding the supporting documents.*

"Plans are nothing;
Planning is everything."
Dwight D. Eisenhower

Ultimate BUSINESS PLANNING
For Visionary Start-Ups & Revolutionary Companies

EXECUTIVE SUMMARY

The executive summary is a one- or two-page synopsis of the entire business plan. The objective of the executive summary is to answer critical questions about the business, while enticing the reader to review the entire plan. As previously stated, the executive summary is usually written last, after all the sections of the plan have been completed.

Company Background

The executive summary begins with the company background. The background informs the reader where your company is headquartered, how long your company has been in business, what products and services your company provides and where your company operates, markets and sells its products and services.

Sample Company Background

Meridian Widgets, Inc., (MWI), was founded in 2005 by John Doe. Headquartered in New Orleans, Louisiana, MWI is a manufacturer and distributor or widgets for industrial, construction and consumer applications. MWI has manufacturing facilities in New Orleans, LA and Flint, MI, and wholesales widgets to home improvement and hardware stores throughout North America and directly to consumers online.

My Company's Background

_____

_____

_____

_____

_____

_____

_____

_____

_____

_____

Ultimate **BUSINESS PLANNING**
For Visionary Start-Ups & Revolutionary Companies

Products and Services Summary
List and describe each product and service you manufacture, distribute, and sell. Briefly discuss how your products and services are:

1.) New;
2.) An improvement to existing products or services;
3.) Better than your competitors;
4.) Innovative; and/or
5.) Unique.

Include pictures of your products and services to enhance your business plan.

Sample Products and Services Summary

MWI manufactures widgets for three segments of the widget market. Our Industrial Widgets are manufactured for use in industrial manufacturing facilities. Our Deluxe Widgets are manufactured for use in heavy and light commercial construction. Our Standard Widgets are manufactured for non-commercial consumer applications such as home improvement projects. Our innovative widget design and manufacturing processes make our widgets twice as durable as our nearest competitor and come with a lifetime guarantee.

My Company's Products and Services Summary

_____

_____

_____

_____

_____

_____

_____

_____

_____

_____

_____

*"To succeed in business,
it is necessary to make others
see things as you see them."*
Aristotle Onassis

Notes and Worksheet Page

Ultimate BUSINESS PLANNING
For Visionary Start-Ups & Revolutionary Companies

Mission Statement

Your company's mission statement is a statement of intent that conveys to the reader, in a clear and concise manner, why your company exists, who your customers are and what products and services your company provides.

Your mission statement helps your company operate within its **core competencies** for the benefit of your employees, customers and other stakeholders.

Core Competencies (def.)
*The strengths of a company that give the company a **competitive advantage**, (Page 73) over its competitors.*

Sample Mission Statement

MWI is dedicated to manufacturing and distributing the highest quality widgets in North American through our commitment to providing exceptional workmanship, sales and service to our customers.

---

*TIP! Perform an internet search for **mission statements** to find additional samples.*

My Company's Mission Statement

_____

_____

_____

_____

_____

_____

_____

_____

_____

_____

_____

Vision Statement

Your company's vision statement should describe to the reader what kind of company you want to build over time.

Your vision statement is an idealized view of what you want your company to be in the future. Your vision statement should be a driving force behind every business objective and business strategy you establish for your company.

Sample Vision Statement

MWI's vision is to be the #1 widget manufacturer in North America within the next five years.

TIP! Perform an internet search for **vision statements** to find additional samples.

My Company's Vision Statement

_____

_____

_____

_____

_____

_____

_____

_____

_____

_____

_____

_____

_____

Values Statement

Your company's values statement informs the public how your company treats its employees, clients and other stakeholders in the communities in which it operates.

Sample Values Statement

MWI is committed to acting honestly and ethically in all our transactions and dealings. We are committed to treating our employees, clients, suppliers and investors fairly and respectfully and we are dedicated to acting responsibly in the communities in which we work.

We will engage in no transaction that does not benefit everyone involved.

---

*TIP! Perform an internet search for **corporate values statements** to find additional samples.*

My Company's Values Statement

_____

_____

_____

_____

_____

_____

_____

_____

_____

_____

Objectives

An objective is a specific short-term, mid-term or long-term outcome you want your company to achieve.

- Short-Term Objective < 90-Days
- 91-Days ≥ Mid-Term Objective ≤ 12-Months
- Long-Term Objective > 12-Months

Effective objectives contain three key elements:

1. An observable and measurable goal;
2. The conditions under which the goal is achieved; and
3. The time-frame for achieving the goal.

Objectives typically focus company efforts on things like increasing sales and market share or decreasing expenses. For example, increasing the number of units sold or the number of clients and decreasing overhead and distribution expenses.

Sample Objectives

1. *Increase our company's client base from 50 to 200 clients within the next 12-months.*
2. *Decrease overhead expenses 20% by the end of FY-2.*
3. *Increase sales from $2,000,000.00 to over $7,500,000.00 by the end of FY-3.*

My Company's Objectives

_____

_____

_____

_____

_____

_____

_____

_____

_____

Start-Up or Expansion Cost Summary and Table

The start-up or expansion cost summary briefly describes the non-recurring costs associated with setting-up shop for the first time, buying an existing business or expanding a business. A start-up or expansion cost table, **Table 4**, accompanies the summary and identifies the sources and uses of funding for start-up or expansion.

Sample Expansion Costs Summary and Table

MWI is investing $20,000.00 along with a bank loan of $100,000.00 to purchase state-of-the industry manufacturing equipment and software to begin production of our new X-Widget. The Expansion Cost table, below, details the sources and uses of funds and the resulting working capital balance.

Table 4: Start-Up or Expansion Cost Table

SOURCES OF EXPANSION CAPITAL	AMOUNT
Owner's Investment	$20,000.00
Bank Loan	$100,000.00
Total Expansion Capital	**$120,000.00**
EXPANSION EXPENSES	
Computers and Software	$15,000.00
Website and Supplies	$5,000.00
Legal and Consulting Expenses	$10,000.00
Purchase New Widget Manufacturing Equipment	**$49,849.51**
Miscellaneous Expansion Expenses	$2,500.00
Total Expansion Expenses	**$82,349.51**
WORKING CAPITAL BALANCE	**$37,650.49**

New Widget Equipment Cost	
Machinery	$42,350.03
Delivery	$ 2,465.37
Installation	$ 4,034.11
Staff Training	$ 1,000.00
TOTAL COST	**$49,849.51**

Working capital balance, for expansion or start-up, equals total start-up or expansion capital ($120,000.00) minus total start-up or expansion expenses ($82,349.51).

Ultimate BUSINESS PLANNING
For Visionary Start-Ups & Revolutionary Companies

My Company's Start-Up or Expansion Costs Summary and Table

_____

_____

_____

_____

_____

_____

_____

_____

SOURCES OF START-UP OR EXPANSION CAPITAL	AMOUNT
Total Start-Up or Expansion Capital	
START-UP OR EXPANSION EXPENSES	
Total Start-Up or Expansion Expenses	
WORKING CAPITAL BALANCE AT START-UP OR EXPANSION	

Ultimate BUSINESS PLANNING
For Visionary Start-Ups & Revolutionary Companies

Pro Forma Sales Graph

Now that you have informed bankers or investors how much it will cost to start or grow your business, you should provide a visual example of how that investment will contribute to increasing revenue for your company. This is done with pro forma sales graph for the corresponding years of your business plan.

Chart 1 shows revenues by product for the next three years. **Chart 2** shows total annual sales for the next three years. The pro forma sales graph is completed after you have completed your sales projections later in the business planning process.

Chart 1: Sample Pro Forma Sales by Product for MWI

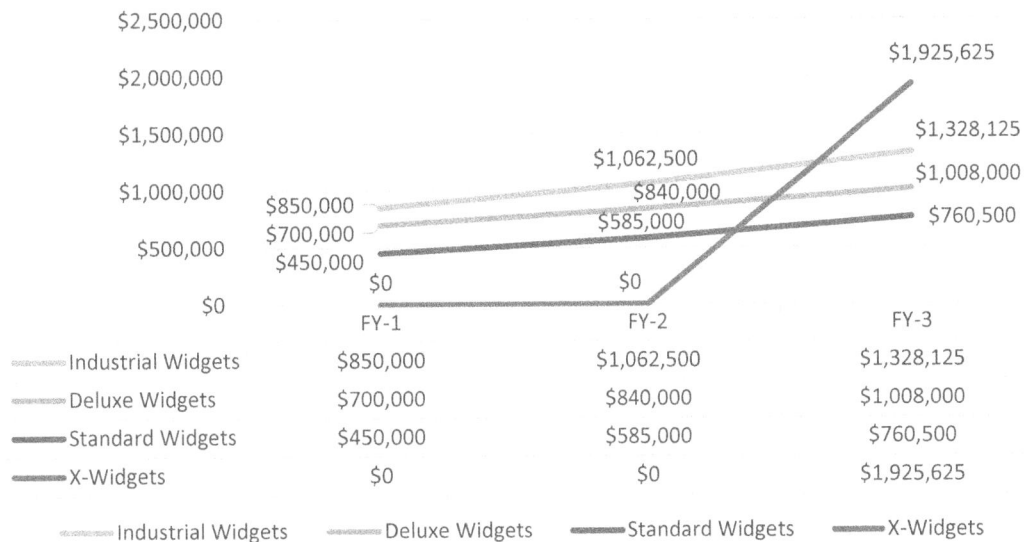

	FY-1	FY-2	FY-3
Industrial Widgets	$850,000	$1,062,500	$1,328,125
Deluxe Widgets	$700,000	$840,000	$1,008,000
Standard Widgets	$450,000	$585,000	$760,500
X-Widgets	$0	$0	$1,925,625

Chart 2: Sample Pro Forma Annual Sales for MWI

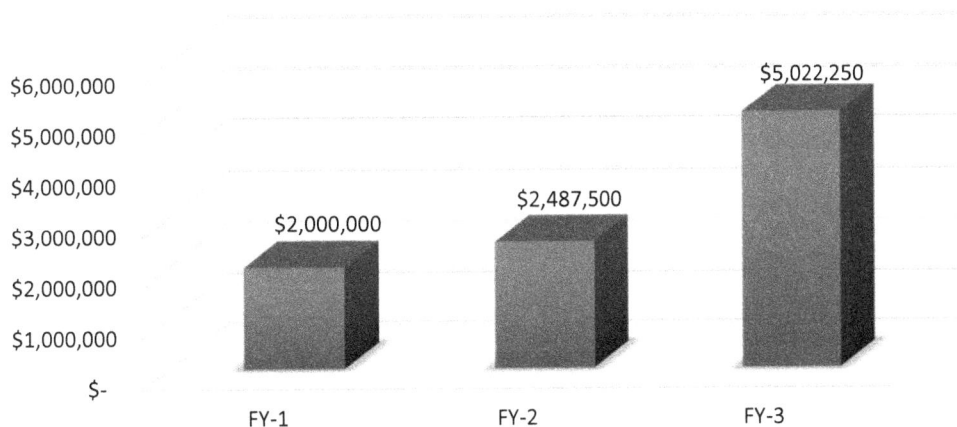

	FY-1	FY-2	FY-3
	$2,000,000	$2,487,500	$5,022,250

39

Keys to Success

Keys to success are those positive influences that help your company achieve its mission, vision and objectives. For example, obtaining a seven-year term for a $100,000.00 business loan as opposed to a five-year term is a key to success because the savings will improve monthly cash flow.

Loan Amount: $100,000.00		7-Year Loan	5-Year Loan
Interest Rate: 10%			
Monthly Payment		$1,660.12	$2,215.70
Monthly Savings/Increased Cash Flow		$464.58	None

For a small business, the additional cash each month can mean the difference between success and failure.

Sample Keys to Success

1. *To secure a minimum 7-year loan term on a bank loan.*
2. *Secure an interest rate at or below 10% on a bank loan.*
3. *Secure a patent on our new X-Widget by the end of FY-1.*

My Company's Keys to Success

_____

_____

_____

_____

_____

_____

_____

_____

_____

_____

_____

*"Where there is no vision,
there is no hope."*
George Washington Carver

Notes and Worksheet Page

MANAGEMENT PLAN

Management Plan Summary

The management plan informs the reader how your company is structured, who owns the business, what products and services your company sells, who works for the company and who advises the company. The management plan begins with a summary that includes:

– **Structure and Ownership**
   - Type of company: Corporation, LLC, Partnership, etc.
   - Owners and ownership percentages

– **Locations**
   - Headquarters, manufacturing, distribution, branch and/or retail locations

– **Owners**

– **Key Employees and Staff**

A Board of Directors is known as a Board of Managers in a Limited Liability Company

– **Board of Directors**
   - President
   - Treasurer
   - Secretary
   - Board Members

If you own a single member company, exclude the board of directors or managers

– **Consultants**

Sample Management Plan Summary

MWI, one of North America's leading widget manufacturing companies, is a Louisiana corporation founded in 2005 by John Doe. John Doe is the CEO of MWI and owner of 90% of the company's outstanding shares. Jim Doe and Mary Doe own the remaining 10% of the company's shares. MWI is headquartered in New Orleans, LA, at 2600 London Ave., and maintains manufacturing facilities in New Orleans, LA, and Flint, MI. MWI has an exceptional team of managers, staff and consultants and a highly qualified and engaged board of directors that includes:

Key Employees
Lexi Chan, Chief Operating Officer
Malcolm Edward, Chief Technology Officer
Zoey Marie, Chief Financial Officer

Consultants
E. Hampton, Management Consultant
C. Blouin, CPA
M. Cade, Attorney

Board of Directors
Dr. Dillard, President
Mrs. J. Camille, Treasurer
Mrs. M. Newman, Secretary
Mr. S. Verrett, Board Member
Mr. B. Gilmore, Board Member

43

My Company's Management Plan Summary

_____

_____

_____

_____

_____

_____

_____

_____

_____

If you own a single member corporation or limited liability company indicate "Owner/CEO - 100%"

		Percentage of Ownership in the Company (if any)
Owners		
Owner/CEO	_____	_____ %
Owner	_____	_____ %
Owner	_____	_____ %
Key Employees		
President	_____	_____ %
Chief Operations Officer	_____	_____ %
Chief Financial Officer	_____	_____ %
Chief Technology Officer	_____	_____ %
Key Employee/Title	_____	_____ %
Key Employee/Title	_____	_____ %
Key Employee/Title	_____	_____ %

Board of Directors

President	_____	_____ %
Treasurer	_____	_____ %
Secretary	_____	_____ %
Board Member	_____	_____ %
Board Member	_____	_____ %

Consultants

Every business, large or small, has advisors who are not employees, but who have an impact on the success or failure of the business. Those advisors are known as your **Master Mind Group**.

The Master Mind

"Coordination of knowledge and effort, in a spirit of harmony, between two or more people, for the attainment of a definite purpose."
Napoleon Hill

As a business owner, your Master Mind Group should include:

- Accountant or CPA
- Attorney
- Business Banker
- Insurance Consultant
- Risk Management Consultant
- Human Resources Consultant
- Business Mentor
- Industry, Marketing, Sales, etc.

Consultants	Name and Company
Accountant/CPA	_____
Attorney	_____
Business Banker	_____
Insurance	_____
Risk Management	_____
Human Resources	_____
Business Mentor	_____
Other (Describe)	_____
Other (Describe)	_____

Personnel Plan and Table

The personnel plan describes the size of your company's workforce and the projected cost to staff the company. **Table 5**, *Personnel Plan Table*, provides the details of the number of workers per position, their job titles and salaries. You can use a simplified personnel plan table, **Table 6**, for the body of the ultimate business plan and include the detailed table in the financial plan section of the business plan.

Tip! *You should include an estimate for taxes, employee benefits and any other personnel cost with your personnel plan totals. For example, the CEO's FY-1 salary of $80,000 would be documented as $108,000 (36% increase) which includes the CEO's salary, taxes and benefits.*

Sample Personnel Plan

MWI has a workforce of 15 people, with a goal of staffing up to 24 by the beginning of FY-3 to oversee production of our new X-Widget. All of our manufacturing employees must be high school graduates and must complete a 4-month probationary period prior to being hired full time.

Table 5: Sample Personnel Plan Table

Title	Salary	Number	FY-1	FY-2 (+10%)	FY-3 (+10%)	Total
MANAGEMENT						
CEO	$108,000	1	$108,000	$118,800	$130,680	$357,480
V.P.	$75,000	1	$75,000	$82,600	$90,750	$248,350
Finance	$70,000	1	$70,000	$77,000	$84,700	$231,700
IT	$60,000	1	$60,000	$66,000	$72,600	$198,600
Clerical	$40,000	2	$80,000	$88,000	$93,600	$261,600
SUBTOTAL		**6**	**$393,000**	**$432,400**	**$472,330**	**$1,297,730**
MANUFACTURING		FY1; FY2; FY3				
Supervisors	$50,000	1; 1; 2	$50,000	$55,000	$121,000	$226,000
Production	$40,000	8; 10; 16	$320,000	$440,000	$774,400	$1,534,400
SUBTOTAL		**9; 11; 18**	**$370,000**	**$495,000**	**$895,400**	**$1,760,400**
TOTAL		**15; 17; 24**	**$763,000**	**$927,400**	**$1,367,730**	**$3,058,130**

Table 6: Sample Simplified Personnel Plan Table

Title	Number FYs 1; 2; 3	Payroll FY-1	Payroll FY-2	Payroll FY-3	Total
Management	6; 6; 6	$393,000	$432,400	$472,330	$1,297,730
Manufacturing	12; 17; 22	$763,000	$927,400	$1,367,7300	$1,760,400
TOTAL	**15; 17; 24**	**$1,148,000**	**$1,537,800**	**$1,994,080**	**$3,058,130**

My Company's Personnel Plan

_____

_____

_____

_____

_____

_____

_____

_____

_____

_____

_____

_____

_____

_____

_____

_____

Ultimate BUSINESS PLANNING

For Visionary Start-Ups & Revolutionary Companies

My Company's Personnel Plan Table

Title	Salary	Number			Payroll FY-1	Payroll FY-2	Payroll FY-3	Total
		FY-1	FY-2	FY-3				
MANAGEMENT								
SUBTOTAL								
OTHER								
SUBTOTAL								
TOTAL								

My Company's Simplified Personnel Plan Table

Title/Position	NUMBER			Payroll FY-1	Payroll FY-2	Payroll FY-3	Total
	FY1	FY2	FY3				
Total							

Employee Benefit Plans

If you plan to offer employee benefits such as health insurance, life insurance or a 401(k) plan, provide a description of the plans and their estimated costs. You should also explain how the employee benefit plans will help your company attract and retain quality employees. Include copies of employee benefit plan documents in the supporting documents section of the business plan.

Reminder: Include the cost of your employee benefit plans in your personnel cost calculations.

Sample Employee Benefit Plans Statement

Every employee will be provided with health insurance and a term life insurance policy for $50,000 paid by the company. Employees will have an option to contribute to the company's 401(k) plan where the company will match contributions up to 10% of the employee's annual salary. If the company exceeds its annual sales goals by at least 20%, every employee will receive a bonus of up to 10% of his or her salary. We believe that our employee benefit plans offer competitive compensation and will allow MWI to attract and retain quality managers and employees.

My Company's Employee Benefit Plans

_____

_____

_____

_____

_____

_____

_____

_____

_____

_____

_____

SWOT Analysis

SWOT analysis is an <u>objective analysis</u> of the internal strengths and weaknesses and external opportunities and threats that affect your company's ability to succeed.

Strengths
Weaknesses
Opportunities
Threats

Objective Analysis (def.)
Honest investigation based on facts, not opinions.

Strengths and Weaknesses

When you analyze your company's strengths and weaknesses, you uncover how well your company is operating with its current human, capital, time and other resources.

> *Tip!* The owners and management team should always be listed as a strength.

- When you analyze your company's strengths, ask, *"What makes our company great?"*
- When you analyze your company's weaknesses, ask, *"What is holding our company back?"*

Opportunities and Threats

When you analyze your company's opportunities and threats, you uncover how your company is affected by external factors that are out of your company's control. Political unrest in foreign markets and fluctuating fuel costs are examples of external factors that can affect your company's bottom-line that are out of your company's control.

- When considering your company's opportunities, ask, *"What can make our company better?"*
- When considering your company's threats, ask, *"What can impede our company's success?"*

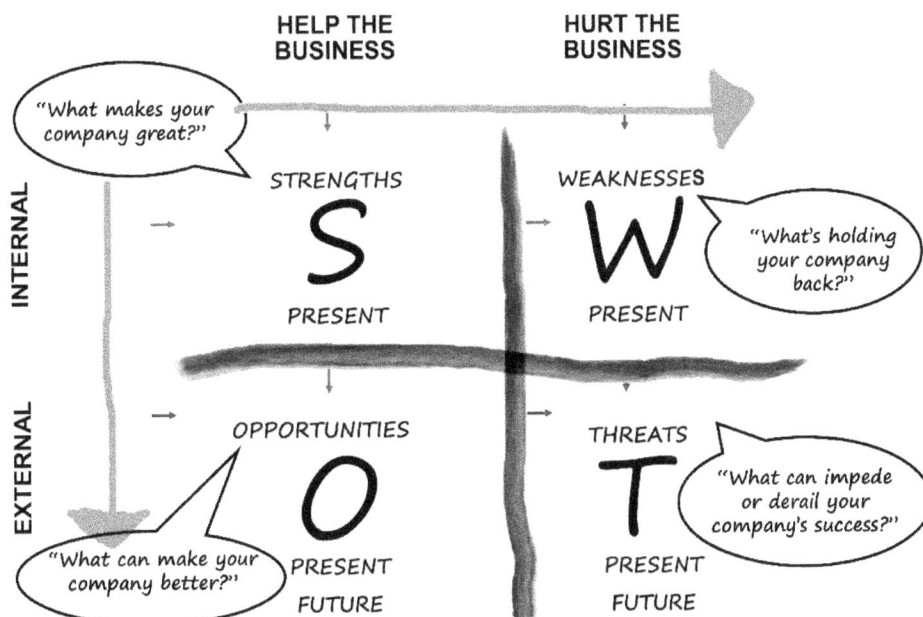

Ultimate BUSINESS PLANNING
For Visionary Start-Ups & Revolutionary Companies

Sample SWOT Analysis

STRENGTHS
- Management
- Products
- Experience

WEAKNESSES
- Access to Capital
- Marketing
- Distribution

OPPORTUNITIES
- Aerospace Market
- Licensing

THREATS
- Rising Costs of Production
- Chinese Widget Manufacturers

My Company's SWOT Analysis

Strengths	Weaknesses

Opportunities	Threats

Why is SWOT Analysis in the Management Plan?

Most business planning books include SWOT analysis in the marketing plan section of the business plan. However, it is included in the management plan section in this workbook for the following reasons:

1. It allows you to remind the reader, throughout the business plan, of your company's strengths;

2. It allows you to explain to the reader, throughout the business plan, how your company will overcome weaknesses;

3. It allows you to expound, throughout the business plan, on how your company will take advantage of opportunities; and

4. It allows you to describe, throughout the business plan, how you will mitigate and manage threats to your company.

Ultimate **BUSINESS PLANNING**

For Visionary Start-Ups & Revolutionary Companies

Notes and Worksheet Page

Milestones

Milestones are measurable, observable and date specific deadlines designed to hold team members accountable for achieving the company's objectives.

Milestones help keep the coordination, planning and execution of your ultimate business plans moving forward. Milestones should be presented in their order of priority, from the first milestone that needs to be achieved to the last. For example, before you get a business loan for $100,000.00, you must write a business plan and fill out a business loan application, so writing the business plan and completing the loan application would be listed before the milestone of getting the loan.

Table 7 is a sample milestones table for MWI. You can include a brief statement or introduction to your milestones, explaining why they are important.

Sample Milestones

MWI has identified several milestones to improve accountability and keep our team's expansion plan on track. Our milestones include:

Table 7: Sample Milestones Table

Task	Start Date	End Date	By
Write a business plan	01/07/20	02/20/20	Owner
Research lenders and apply for a loan	02/21/20	03/25/20	CFO
Secure a $100K loan or investment	03/26/20	06/18/20	Owner
Purchase and install the new widget equipment	07/01/20	07/11/20	COO
Train the staff to operate new widget equipment	07/11/20	11/15/20	Plant Manager
Begin producing X-Widgets	11/17/20	Ongoing Activity	Owners and staff

Ultimate **BUSINESS PLANNING**

For Visionary Start-Ups & Revolutionary Companies

My Company's Milestones

Task	Start Date	End Date	By

Exit Strategy

An exit strategy- *the method by which a business owner or investor recoups capital invested or transfers ownership in a business-* is determined by the objectives of the business owners and investors. Developing an exit strategy at start-up helps owners, employees and investors work towards building value in the business from day one.

In this section, discuss the method by which you plan to transfer ownership in the business or how your investors plan to recoup their investment in the business at a future point in time. Some exit strategy examples include:

Owner's Exit Strategy Objectives	Investor's Exit Strategy Objectives
• Transfer ownership to the children, business partners or employees	• Obtain financing from a venture capital fund
• Refinance debt or buy back shares to buy out investors	• Sell stock in the business through an **Initial Public Offering (IPO)**
• Sell the business and retire	• Sell the business

Initial Public Offering (def.)
Shares of stock in a company are offered for sale to the general public for the first time.

Sample Exit Strategy

Once MWI achieves its vision of being the #1 widget company in North American, John Doe will begin to transfer 51% of the company's outstanding stock to his children and sell the remaining 39% of his shares in the company to the minority owners.

My Company's Exit Strategy

_____

_____

_____

_____

_____

_____

_____

Ultimate BUSINESS PLANNING
For Visionary Start-Ups & Revolutionary Companies

Notes and Worksheet Page

PRODUCTS AND SERVICES

A business does not exist without products and services to sell.

Products and Services Summary
In clear, concise and straightforward language, describe your company's products and services and why customers will buy them. Your products and services summary should include an overview of the **features** and **benefits** of your products and services.

Features (def.)
Characteristics of your product or service that describe its appearance, components and/or capabilities.

Example of a Product Feature
MWI's 100% aluminum widgets weigh 40% less than traditional steel widgets.

Benefits (def.)
An advantage your product or service has over its competitors.

Example of a Product Benefit
The lighter weight of MWI's aluminum widgets result in a 45% increase in performance and stability, allowing the company the ability to offer the only lifetime warranty in the widget industry.

If you own a business that sells hundreds or thousands of products or services, describe them in categories or groups. For example, Debonair Clothier, a retail men's store, might describe the 200 shirts it sells in the categories: *Dress Shirts*, *T-Shirts* and *Casual Shirts*.

Sample Products and Services Summary

MWI manufactures widgets for three segments of the widget market. Our Industrial Widgets are manufactured for use in industrial manufacturing facilities. Our Deluxe Widgets are manufactured for use in heavy and light commercial construction. Our Standard Widgets are manufactured for non-commercial consumer applications such as home improvement projects.

MWI's 100% aluminum widgets weigh 40% less than traditional steel widgets. The lighter weight of MWI's aluminum widgets result in a 45% increase in performance and stability, allowing the company the ability to offer the only lifetime warranty in the widget industry. MWI is also developing the new X-Widget for use in the aerospace industry. The X-Widget will be the most advanced widget ever designed for aerospace applications and will help MWI double revenues by the end of FY-3.

My Company's Products and Services Summary

_____

_____

_____

_____

_____

_____

_____

_____

_____

_____

_____

_____

_____

_____

_____

_____

Patents, Trademarks and Copyrights

Patents, trademarks and copyrights provide exclusive rights to manufacture, distribute or sell a product or service.

Patents provide a patent owner limited legal monopoly granted to an individual or firm to make, use and sell its invention and to exclude others from doing so without permission. The value of a patent is a business asset that can be used as collateral for a business loan or to secure an investment in your business. For example, in 1997 Steve Jobs convinced Bill Gates to invest $150 million into Apple in exchange for Apple dropping patent infringement lawsuits against Microsoft[1].

A trademark is a distinctive design, graphic, logo, symbol, word or any combination thereof that uniquely identifies a firm and/or its goods or services, guarantees the item's genuineness, and gives its owner the legal rights to the trademark's unauthorized use.

While most trademarks hold little to no tangible value, brands like Coca-Cola and BMW have a great deal of tangible value, known as **goodwill**. Coca-Cola is the world's number 3 ranked global brand with an estimated value over $73 billion and BMW is ranked number 11 with an estimated value over $41.5 billion[2].

Goodwill (def.)
Assumed value of an intangible saleable asset.

A copyright is a legal monopoly that protects published or unpublished original work (for the duration of its author's life plus 50 years) from unauthorized duplication without due credit and compensation. Spotify, a music streaming service, has been plagued by persistent claims of copyright infringement resulting in at least two multi-million-dollar settlements. In 2016, Spotify agreed to pay $30 million to the National Music Publishers' Association[3] and in 2017 Spotify agreed to pay $43 million[4] to settle copyright infringement lawsuits.

The examples presented reveal the potential value of your company's patents, trademarks and copyrights, while also revealing how the unlawful use of another's patent, trademark or copyright can cost your company a great deal of money.

Sample Patents, Trademarks and Copyrights Statement

MWI maintains patents for each of its widget designs and has applied for a provisional patent for our new X-Widget. MWI has a trademark for the company's logo and our CEO has published several trade publications for the widget industry, including the research paper, Widget Design Applications for the Aerospace Industry.

---

[1] Source: Forbes.com
[2] Source: Interbrand's annual Best Global Brands ranking.
[3] Source: Billboard.com
[4] Source: Forbes.com

Ultimate **BUSINESS PLANNING**

For Visionary Start-Ups & Revolutionary Companies

My Company's Patents, Trademarks and Copyrights

_____

_____

_____

_____

_____

_____

_____

_____

_____

_____

_____

_____

_____

_____

_____

Licensing and Franchise Agreements

A licensing agreement is a written contract under which the owner (licensor) of a copyright, trademark, servicemark or other intellectual property allows another party (licensee) to use, make or sell copies of the original. For example, The Walt Disney Company's Consumer Products and Interactive segment had revenue of $1.1 billion in the 3rd quarter of FY-2016, of which 68% ($748 million) was earned from product licensing.

A franchise agreement is a legal contract in which a business (franchisor) consents to provide its brand, business model and management support to another party (franchisee) that allows the franchisee to set up and run a similar business in exchange for a fee and a share of the income generated. One of the world's most recognized franchises is McDonald's, which has over 36,000 franchised locations in 120 countries.

If your company has a licensing agreement or franchise agreement to sell another company's products and services or your company offers licensing agreements or franchise agreements for others to sell your company's products and services, discuss the details in this section.

Sample Licensing and Franchise Agreements Statement

MWI does not have or offer any licensing or franchise agreements for its widget products. As we expand into the aerospace industry with our new X-Widget, we will consider offering licensing agreements to international widget manufacturers in South American and Europe.

My Company's Licensing and Franchise Agreements

_____

_____

_____

_____

_____

_____

_____

_____

Future Products and Services

Before you complete this section, review *Growth Strategies 101* on page 13. If you know the growth strategy or products and services your company plans to offer in the future (after the first year), describe them and their impact on your company's growth in this section. If you do not have any future products and services planned at this time, state so.

Keep in mind that your ultimate business plan is a living document. You should update your plans regularly, especially when you decide on the strategies, products and services you will use to grow your company.

Sample Future Products and Services Statement

MWI is in the final stages of development of the X-Widget. The X-Widget is designed for use in the aerospace industry and will be available for sale by the beginning of FY-3. MWI will concentrate efforts on launching the X-Widget and meeting the sales projections in this business plan before considering any other growth strategies.

My Company's Future Products and Services

_____

_____

_____

_____

_____

_____

_____

_____

Ultimate BUSINESS PLANNING
For Visionary Start-Ups & Revolutionary Companies

MARKETING PLAN

Your marketing plan encompasses all the activities it takes to get a product or service in the hands of consumers. Marketing is so critical to the overall success of the business that you may want to write a separate, more comprehensive marketing plan in addition to your ultimate business plan.

Your marketing plan is based on the **"4Ps" Marketing Mix** which includes:

- **Product.** A product is a tangible good or an intangible service a company sells to satisfy a customer's needs or wants to generate revenue for the company.

- **Price.** Price includes all the activities involved in determining the optimum selling price for a product or service. Cost of production, packaging, distribution, profit margin, marketing and more will all impact the final price of a product or service.

- **Promotion.** Promotion includes all the methods used to spread the word to consumers about your products and services such as internet, radio and TV ads.

- **Place.** Place includes the plans created by management that specify how products and services will reach consumers and where products and services will be sold.

"When product, price, promotion and place are effectively blended, they form a marketing program that provides want-satisfying goods and services for the company's market."

Management of a Sales Force
By Rosann L. Spiro, Gregory A. Rich and William J. Stanton

Ultimate **BUSINESS PLANNING**

For Visionary Start-Ups & Revolutionary Companies

Market Analysis Summary

Your marketing plan begins with a market analysis summary that provides the reader an overview of the market for your products and services. The market analysis summary lays the groundwork for your marketing plan, explaining how your company will utilize its strengths and opportunities to capitalize on the market opportunity and win market share.

Sample Market Analysis Summary

The North American market for widgets has grown an average of 15% per year for the past five years because of new construction spending exceeding $700 billion annually in the U.S and $200 billion annually in Canada. Infrastructure spending in North American is projected to continue double digit growth for the next ten years, creating an ongoing demand for widgets.

The market for aerospace widgets is in its infancy because of new private space exploration companies. The new aerospace widget market is estimated at $50 billion annually. MWI will capitalize on the growing industry with the introduction of our patent-pending X-Widget by FY-3.

My Company's Market Analysis Summary

_____

_____

_____

_____

_____

_____

_____

_____

_____

_____

_____

*"I never dreamed about success.
I worked for it."*

Estée Lauder

Notes and Worksheet Page

Market Segmentation

Subdividing a large group, like all widget users, into smaller groups with similar characteristics and needs is known as market segmentation.

Markets are often segmented by age, race, sex, income, habits (For example, smokers and non-smokers), hobbies, industry and education level. Examples of market segments include:

CLOTHING	CELL PHONES	ADULTS	TRANSPORTATION	WIDGETS
Men	Android	65+	Car drivers	Industrial
Women	Apple iOS	55-64	Motorcycle drivers	Deluxe
Girls	Windows	46-54	Scooter drivers	Standard
Boys		36-45	Bicycle riders	Aerospace
		26-35	Bus riders	Other
		18-35		

In this section, provide a breakdown of the unique segments of the market for your products and services. The information you provide is based on the research you should have already conducted about the market for your products and services. You should include a chart, similar to **Chart 3** below, to illustrate the breakdown of your industry's market segments.

Sample Market Segmentation

The market for widgets in North America is 20 million units annually and is divided into five main segments, with the largest segment being the standard widgets segment. MWI markets its widgets to the three largest segments of the widget market and plans to expand to the fourth largest segment, the aerospace widget market, by FY-3.

Chart 3: North American Widget Market Segmentation

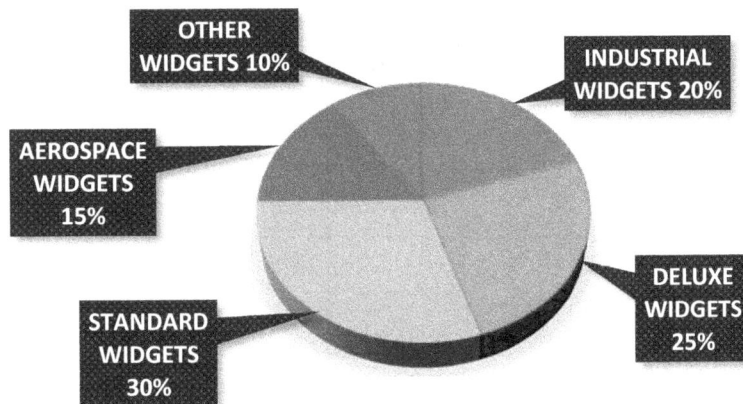

My Company's Market Segmentation

_____

_____

_____

_____

_____

_____

_____

_____

_____

_____

_____

_____

Market Segmentation Table (Optional)
Use the data to create a pie chart like the one on the previous page.

Segment	Segments defined in above (For example, Segment 4: Other Widgets)			
	1	**2**	**3**	**4**
Size ($)				
Size (units)				
Projected Annual Growth (%)				

Target Market Analysis

Target market analysis differentiates the characteristics of the segments of the market at which the marketing campaign is focused.

In our example, MWI is currently focusing marketing efforts on three differentiated segments of the widget market. Therefore, the objective of our target market analysis is to answer, at a minimum, four questions:

1. Why are we targeting those segments of the market?
2. Who are the potential customers for each segment of the market?
3. What is our company's **value proposition** for each segment of the market?
4. How do we expect demand for our products and services to grow in each segment of the market over the next three years?

Value Proposition (def.)
The reasons a customer will buy a company's products and services.

Sample Target Market Analysis

MWI began by fabricating custom widgets for the commercial construction industry. Within two years, management had learned more about the market for widgets and set in motion a plan to manufacture widgets for the largest segments of the widget market to maximize the opportunity for long-term growth. As a result, MWI expanded into the manufacture of our brand of industrial widgets, deluxe widgets and standard widgets.

- *For the industrial widget segment of the market, MWI will focus marketing efforts on specific companies with specific needs and opportunities. Customization is the value proposition we will offer this segment of the market. Based on our research, we expect the market for industrial widgets to grow at 15% per year over the next three years.*

- *For the deluxe widget segment of the market, MWI will focus marketing efforts on commercial construction and heavy construction customers. Durability, quality and a product warranty are the value propositions we will offer this segment of the market. Based on our research, we expect the market for deluxe widgets to grow at 20% per year over the next three years.*

- *For the standard widget market, MWI will focus marketing efforts on customers seeking widgets for a variety of non-commercial consumer applications. Variety and low cost are the value propositions we will offer this segment of the market. Based on our research, we expect the market for standard widgets to grow at 10% per year over the next three years.*

Ultimate BUSINESS PLANNING
For Visionary Start-Ups & Revolutionary Companies

My Company's Target Market Analysis

_____
_____
_____
_____
_____
_____
_____
_____
_____
_____
_____
_____
_____
_____
_____
_____
_____
_____
_____
_____
_____
_____
_____
_____

Market Trend Analysis

Market trend analysis utilizes market research to determine the general direction in which the market for your products and services is developing or changing and how those developments or changes impact your business.

On Market Trends
*"Any customer can have a car painted any color he wants
as long as it's black."*
Henry Ford

Henry Ford failed to see the trend in the marketplace towards consumers wanting the option to pick the color of a car, which allowed other manufacturers like Chrysler, Dodge and Cadillac to take a portion of market share away from Ford.

Knowing the market trends that affect your target markets, helps your company:

1. Prepare for changes in the market that could negatively affect your company;
2. Take advantage of changes in the market that could positively affect your company; and
3. Establish or maintain your **competitive advantage** in the marketplace.

> **Competitive Advantage (def.)**
> *An advantage a company has over its competitors, allowing it to generate greater sales, better margins and/or more customers.*

Examples of Market Trends[5]

- Changing customer needs, such as increasing or decreasing product or service usage;
- Changing demographics, such as the trend for children to stay at home longer;
- Pricing, such as a market trend to discounting;
- Technology, such as the increasing use of online purchasing;
- Economy, such as interest rate changes;
- Communication/Media, such as the increased use of social media by certain customers; and
- Cyclical trends, such as how housing demands will affect the construction market.

WIDGET MARKET TREND ANALYSIS

---

[5] Source: **www.M4BMarketing.com**, *What Marketing Trends are Affecting Your Small Business* by Susan Oakes.

Sample Market Trend Analysis

Advances in manufacturing, technology and design have created new opportunities for widget applications in the aerospace industry. The emerging aerospace market is estimated at $50 billion annually, with growth rates projected up to 25% a year for the next ten years. MWI will take advantage of the aerospace industry opportunity with the introduction of the company's X-Widget.

As trends in the widget industry continue to shift away from a 45% dependence on the construction industry, MWI's research team will continue to be an industry leader in developing and supplying widgets for new and emerging markets.

My Company's Market Trend Analysis

_____

_____

_____

_____

_____

_____

_____

_____

_____

Marketing Strategy

Marketing strategy applies the results of your market analysis to coordinate, plan and execute specific actions- advertising, publicity, branding, social media campaigns, etc.- designed to reach customers and increase sales.

After conducting a thorough analysis of the market, you should be ready to develop a comprehensive strategy for marketing your products and services to potential customers. Begin this section with a brief overview of the human, capital and other resources you will dedicate to marketing and the impact those resources will have on increasing your sales or market share. You should include a short marketing budget that details where your company will spend its marketing dollars.

Sample Marketing Strategy

MWI's marketing strategy will focus on improving brand awareness through a combination of paid radio, TV and print advertising and free social media marketing and publicity. We will budget at least $300,000.00 over the next 18-months towards implementing our marketing strategy.

Each of our target market segments will be aligned with an effective combination of advertising and publicity to support our sales team. While each target market will require a unique marketing strategy, each will be designed to maximize the sales, market share and profit targets we have established in this business plan.

MWI's management team recognizes the limitations of our experience, therefore we will hire a marketing consultant or firm to design and execute our marketing plans.

Table 8: MWI's proposed marketing budget through the end of FY-3.

Marketing Budget Item	Estimated Cost
Marketing consultant/firm	$70,000
TV advertising campaigns	$110,000
Radio advertising campaigns	$40,000
Internet advertising campaigns	$30,000
Social media marketing campaigns	$20,000
Sponsorships and other campaigns	$30,000
TOTAL	**$300,000**

Tip! *A detailed marketing plan would detail the specific budget and strategy for each target market. For example, MWI will spend $15,000.00 on print advertising in Widget World Magazine and Industry Today, to reach potential industrial widget customers. The print ads will serve as a lead-in for our industrial widget sales force to cold call potential new clients.*

Ultimate BUSINESS PLANNING
For Visionary Start-Ups & Revolutionary Companies

My Company's Marketing Strategy

_____
_____
_____
_____
_____
_____
_____
_____
_____
_____
_____
_____
_____
_____
_____
_____
_____
_____

Marketing Budget Item	Estimated Cost
Total	

*"Anyone can steer the ship,
but it takes a leader to chart the course."*
John C. Maxwell

Ultimate BUSINESS PLANNING
For Visionary Start-Ups & Revolutionary Companies

Notes and Worksheet Page

WEBSITE PLAN AND SOCIAL MEDIA PLANS

Website Plan

In today's globally competitive environment, a website is, in many ways, more essential than a business card. In fact, your website is the online business card for your company. A great website can make a one-person company appear as large as a multi-national conglomerate.

In other words, if you own a business, you need a website.

Your company's website should include information about your company, the products and services your company sells and a way for visitors to contact your company. If your company sells products over the internet, your website should also include e-commerce capabilities.

The first step in developing a website is securing a website name. If the name of your business is already in use by another company, you will need to find another name that "fits" your business and that your clients can easily remember or find via an internet search.

The next step is to determine your website's content. Website content typically includes, but is not limited to, the following:

- Articles
- Banner ads
- Blog
- Newsletter

- Affiliate links
- Downloadable brochure
- E-commerce shopping cart
- Contact information

- FAQs
- Events
- Videos
- Pictures

Sample Website Plan

MWI's website will included the following pages:

- ***Home Page:*** *Includes information about our company's background;*
- ***Products Page:*** *Includes information and pictures of our industrial, deluxe and standard widgets, as well as information on our upcoming X-Widget;*
- ***E-Commerce Store:*** *Includes our widget products for sale online; and*
- ***Contact Us:*** *Allows customers and potential customers to contact call us or send us an e-mail with any questions or comments.*

MWI will hire a consultant to build our new website and to ensure the site appears in the top search results for widgets by increasing the site's visibility in search engines, known as search engine optimization.

Ultimate BUSINESS PLANNING

For Visionary Start-Ups & Revolutionary Companies

My Company's Website Plan

Check the pages and content that will be included in your website:

☐ Landing page   ☐ Home page   ☐ Testimonials
☐ Home page   ☐ E-commerce store   ☐ Downloadable brochure
☐ About the company   ☐ Contact us page   ☐ Other downloadable content
☐ Products and services   ☐ Videos   ☐ Calendar of events
☐ Media/news room   ☐ Picture gallery   ☐ Blog or newsletter
☐ Mailing list sign-up   ☐ Other page or content (describe below)

_____

_____

_____

_____

_____

_____

_____

_____

_____

_____

_____

_____

_____

_____

_____

Social Media Plan

Your social media plan describes how your company will utilize social media platforms like Facebook, Twitter and Instagram to build brand awareness.

As a critical component of your overall marketing strategy, your social media plan helps your company interact with clients, it keeps clients informed about your company's products and services and it can generate buzz, leads and new clients.

To be successful, your social media plan must contain five key elements, known as the **"5Cs" of Social Media Marketing**. The "5Cs" include:

Content
You must create and share content that focuses on your costumer's needs, wants and interests. For example, if your company makes widgets for high-performance cars, you can start a YouTube channel that reviews new sports cars that utilize your company's widgets.

Conversations
You must monitor and respond to customer questions and comments and encourage your clients to share their wants, needs and thoughts. Online surveys are a great way to engage your customers and stimulate conversations.

Community
You must encourage clients and experts to share their knowledge and add value to your content and conversations. Blogs and online forums are proven methods of building an engaged social media community.

Connections
You must find out where your customers and experts share, listen and spend time on the internet and connect with them to help spread your message. Adding a link from your website to an expert's blog or retweeting a customer's post can help build connections.

Consistent
Managing your social media plan requires a consistent effort. For example, you can assign a staff member to post weekly updates to your company's blog about widgets.

Sample Social Media Plan

MWI will engage potential clients via social media by employing the following social media strategies:

- *Daily Twitter posts about our widgets and how they are used by our clients;*
- *Weekly Facebook posts on trends in the widget industry; and*
- *Monthly YouTube video posts about how to use our widgets.*

My Company's Social Media Plan

_____

_____

_____

_____

_____

_____

_____

_____

_____

_____

_____

_____

_____

_____

_____

_____

_____

_____

#WIDGETS

"Keep going,
no matter what."
Reginald Lewis

Ultimate BUSINESS PLANNING

For Visionary Start-Ups & Revolutionary Companies

Notes and Worksheet Pages

SALES PLAN

Sales Plan Summary:
Sales objectives and the strategies for achieving them.

Sales plan tables, in units (Table 2) and annual sales (Table 3), were introduced on page 18. Sales plan charts, by product (Chart 1) and annual sales (Chart 2), were introduced on page 39. The one component of the sales plan section of the business plan that has not been discussed is the *Sales Plan Summary*.

The sales plan summary describes the company's sales strategy, explains how they are achievable with the company's current resources and the strategies the company plans to implement to achieve the sales targets over the next three years.

Sample Sales Plan Summary

MWI's sales success depends on our exceptional sales team's deep expertise in selling customers on the features and benefits of MWI widgets. MWI's strategy to demonstrate real world applications for our widgets will help us continue to have an industry-leading client closing rate of 80% and easily achieve both our unit sales and gross revenue sales targets during FYs 1-3. Furthermore, the company's $300,000.00 investment in marketing will provide the support necessary to achieve and likely exceed the sales targets in this business plan.

- *(Optional) Table 2 or Chart 1*
- *(Optional) Table 3 or Chart 2*

My Company's Sales Plan Summary

_____

_____

_____

_____

_____

_____

_____

_____

_____

_____

_____

Ultimate BUSINESS PLANNING

For Visionary Start-Ups & Revolutionary Companies

Notes and Worksheet Page

FINANCIAL PLAN

If your business idea is enticing enough to gain preliminary buy-in from bankers and investors, you are halfway to getting the financing you need. However, what bankers and investors really want to see is a realistic and achievable financial plan that shows how your company will:

1. Use a bank loan or investment to grow the company; and
2. Earn enough revenue to repay a bank loan or investment.

The answers to those questions, and more, lie in your financial plan. Your financial plan provides the numerical details that prove your idea is viable and a good risk.

Financial Plan Summary

Your financial plan begins with the financial plan summary. The financial plan summary is a brief introduction about your funding needs and the increase in sales, profits or market share that will be generated if you get the money you are seeking.

The summary should include a brief description of the assumptions your team is making about the cost of capital, business tax rates, an investor's funding terms and other information that might impact revenue and expenses. The summary should also discuss the types of financial analyses used in preparing your financial plan.

Sample Financial Plan Summary

MWI is seeking a $100,000.00 bank loan to purchase the equipment required to manufacture the new X-Widget. With the investment, MWI will be able to more than double sales from $2 million in FY-1 to over $5 million by the end of FY-3.

Our general assumptions include:

- *Bank loan interest rate of 8%;*
- *Bank loan term of 7 years (85 months);*
- *Overhead will remain level at 15% per year; and*
- *Our business tax rate will be 35%.*

Our comprehensive financial plan includes:

Expansion Cost Table;	*Pro Forma Profit and Loss Statement;*
Break-Even Point Analysis;	*Pro Forma Cash Flow Statement;*
Pro Forma Sales Forecast;	*Pro Forma Balance Sheet; and*
Pro Forma Profit and Loss Statement;	*Ratio Analysis*

Ultimate BUSINESS PLANNING
For Visionary Start-Ups & Revolutionary Companies

My Company's Financial Plan Summary

Our comprehensive financial plan includes:

☐ Start-Up or Expansion Cost Table
☐ Break-Even Point Analysis
☐ Pro Forma Sales Forecast
☐ Pro Forma Profit and Loss Statement

☐ Pro Forma Cash Flow Statement
☐ Pro Forma Cash Flow Statement
☐ Pro Forma Balance Sheet
☐ Ratio Analysis

☐ Other: _____

☐ Other: _____

_____

_____

_____

_____

_____

_____

_____

_____

_____

_____

_____

_____

_____

_____

_____

_____

_____

_____

_____

_____

_____

Start-Up or Expansion Cost Table

The start-up or expansion cost table details the sources and uses of funds required to start or expand the business. Since the table was explained on page 37, the goal here is to simply reproduce the table from the executive summary and include it in the financial plan.

The summary is not included in in the financial plan.

Sample Expansion Costs Table

Table 5: Start-Up or Expansion Cost Table

SOURCES OF EXPANSION CAPITAL	AMOUNT
Owner's Investment	$20,000.00
Bank Loan	$100,000.00
Total Expansion Capital	**$120,000.00**
EXPANSION EXPENSES	
Computers and Software	$15,000.00
Website and Supplies	$5,000.00
Legal and Consulting Expenses	$10,000.00
Purchase New Widget Manufacturing Equipment	**$49,849.51**
Miscellaneous Expansion Expenses	$2,500.00
Total Expansion Expenses	**$82,349.51**
WORKING CAPITAL BALANCE	**$37,650.49**

New Widget Equipment Cost

Equipment	$42,350.03
Delivery	$ 2,465.37
Installation	$ 4,034.11
Staff Training	$ 1,000.00
TOTAL COST	**$49,849.51**

MERIDIAN

Ultimate BUSINESS PLANNING
For Visionary Start-Ups & Revolutionary Companies

MY Company's Start-Up or Expansion Cost Table

SOURCES OF START-UP OR EXPANSION CAPITAL	AMOUNT
Total Start-Up or Expansion Capital	
TOTAL START-UP OR EXPANSION EXPENSES	
Total Start-Up or Expansion Expenses	
WORKING CAPITAL BALANCE	

Break-Even Point Analysis

The break-even point is the point at which revenue equals expenses, preventing the business from earning a profit or operating at a loss.

In order to calculate the break-even point (BEP), you need to know the **fixed costs** and the **variable costs** it takes to produce your products and services.

Fixed Cost (def.)
A fixed cost is a cost that does not change with an increase or decrease in the amount of goods or services produced or sold. Fixed costs must be paid regardless of the level of business activity.

Examples of Fixed Costs
- Rent
- Insurance
- Internet & Telephone Service

Variable Cost (def.)
A variable cost is a business expense that varies with production output. Variable costs typically rise during an increase in production and decline with a decrease in output.

Examples of Variable Costs
- Parts & Materials
- Production Labor Costs
- Shipping Costs

Illustration of the Break-Even Point

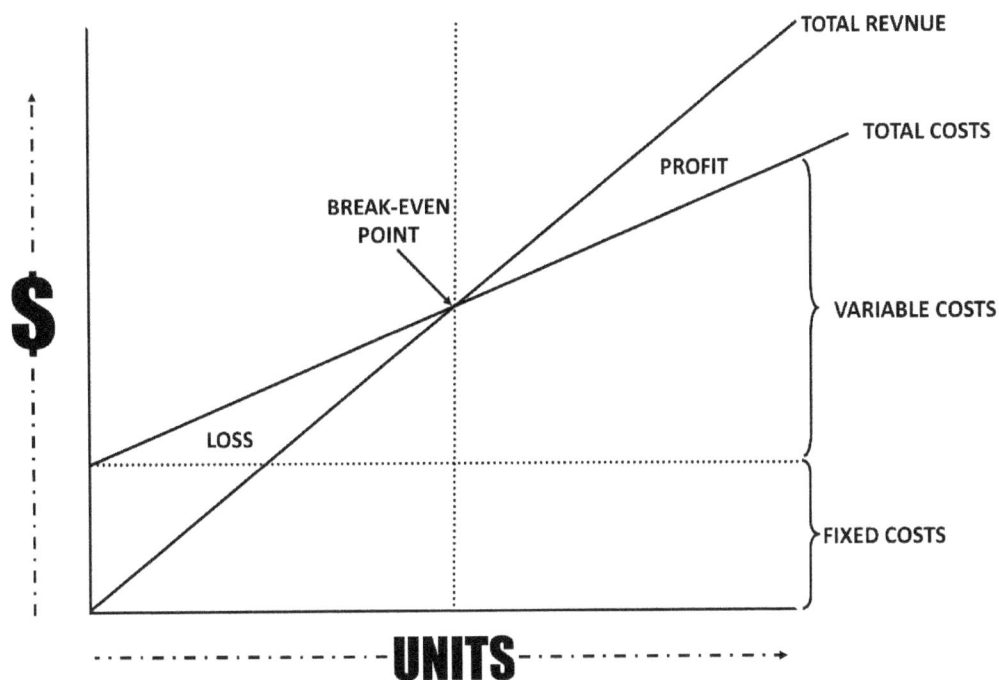

There are two primary methods to calculate the BEP: **Sales Method** and **Units Method**. The sales method is typically used to calculate the BEP for total monthly, quarterly or annual sales. The units method is typically used to determine the BEP for a single product or service.

Break-Even Point by Sales Method

To calculate the BEP using the sales method, divide the company's fixed monthly, quarterly or annual expenses by the company's **contribution margin ratio**.

Contribution Margin Ratio (def.)

Also known as the Gross Profit Percentage, the contribution margin ratio (CMR) is the difference between a company's sales and variable expenses, expressed as a percentage.

Formula

(Sales - Variable Expenses) ÷ Sales = CMR

Calculating the CMR:

Sales = $100,000
Variable Expenses = $70,000
CMR = ($100,000-$70,000) ÷ $100,000
CMR = $30,000 ÷ $100,000
CMR = 30%

The example below illustrates the BEP calculation for MWI using the sales method.

Inputs
- Fixed Expenses: $300,000 (Annually)
- Variable Expenses: 75% of sales or $225,000
- Contribution Margin Ratio: ($300,000 - $225,000) ÷ $300,000 = 25%

BREAK-EVEN POINT CALCULATION

Fixed Expenses	÷	CMR	=	Break-Even Sales
$300,000	÷	25%	=	$1,200,000

BEP: SALES $1,200,000/YEAR

MWI must earn at least $1.2 million a year to break-even.

BEP Using the Units Method

To calculate the BEP using the units method, divide the company's fixed monthly, quarterly or annual expenses for each product or service by the company's contribution margin for each product or service. The example below illustrates the BEP calculation for MWI's industrial widgets using the units method:

Inputs
- Fixed Expenses: $300,000 per year
- Average Selling Price: $8.50 per unit (Industrial widgets)
- Variable Expenses: $2.50 per unit
- Contribution Margin: $6.00 per unit ($8.50-$8.50)

BEP: UNITS 50,000/YEAR

BREAK-EVEN POINT CALCULATION

Fixed Expenses	÷	CMR	=	Break-Even Units
$300,000	÷	$6.00	=	50,000

MWI must sell at least 50,000 industrial widgets a year to break-even.

Ultimate **BUSINESS PLANNING**
For Visionary Start-Ups & Revolutionary Companies

My Company's Break-Even Point Analysis in Sales

Fixed Expenses (FE)	=
Contribution Margin Ratio (CMR)	=
FE ÷ CMR = BEP Sales	

My Company's Break-Even Point Analysis in Units

Fixed Expenses (FE)	=
Per Unit Selling Price (SP)	=
Per Unit Variable Expense (VE)	=
FE ÷ (SP − VE) = BEP Units	

Tip! Use the method that best fits your company.

Ultimate **BUSINESS PLANNING**

For Visionary Start-Ups & Revolutionary Companies

Notes and Worksheet Page

*"The big secret in life is that there is no big secret.
Whatever your goal, you can get there
if you're willing to work."*
Oprah Winfrey

Ultimate **BUSINESS PLANNING**

For Visionary Start-Ups & Revolutionary Companies

Notes and Worksheet Page

Pro Forma Sales Forecast

Input the sales forecast tables, from page 18, here in the financial plan.

Sample Pro Forma Sales Forecast in Units

Product	Unit Sales FY-1	Unit Sales FY-2	Unit Sales FY-3	Total
Industrial Widgets	100,000	125,000 (+25%)	156,250 (+25%)	381,250
Deluxe Widgets	200,000	240,000 (+20%)	288,000 (+20%)	728,000
Standard Widgets	250,000	325,000 (+30%)	422,500 (+30%)	997,500
X-Widgets	----	----	32,500 (New)	32,500
Total	**550,000**	**690,000 (≈25%)**	**900,000**	**2,140,000**

Sample Pro Forma Sales Forecast in Revenue by Product

Product	Selling Price	Revenue FY-1	Revenue FY-2	Revenue FY-3	Total Revenue FYs 1-3
Industrial Widgets	$8.50	$850,000	$1,062,500	$1,328,125	$3,240,625
Deluxe Widgets	$3.50	$700,000	$840,000	$1,008,000	$2,548,000
Standard Widgets	$1.80	$450,000	$585,000	$760,500	$1,795,000
X-Widgets	$59.25	$0	$0	$1,925,625	$1,925,625
Total		**$2,000,000**	**$2,487,500**	**$5,022,250**	**$9,509,750**

Ultimate BUSINESS PLANNING
For Visionary Start-Ups & Revolutionary Companies

My Company's Sales Forecast (Units)

Product	Unit Sales FY-1	Unit Sales FY-2	Unit Sales FY-3	Total
Total				

Ultimate BUSINESS PLANNING

For Visionary Start-Ups & Revolutionary Companies

My Company's Sales Forecast (Revenue by Product)

Product	Selling Price	Revenue FY-1	Revenue FY-2	Revenue FY-3	Total Revenue FYs 1-3
Total					

Ultimate BUSINESS PLANNING
For Visionary Start-Ups & Revolutionary Companies

Notes and Worksheet Pages

Ultimate BUSINESS PLANNING
For Visionary Start-Ups & Revolutionary Companies

Pro Forma Profit and Loss Statement

The Profit and Loss Statement (P&L) is a straightforward accounting of your revenues and expenses during a month, quarter or year. The formula for determining your company's profit or loss during the period is simply:

| Total Revenues |
| - Total Expenses |
| = **Profit or (Loss)** |

*Profits are shown in **black** while losses are shown in parenthesis or red.*

Most businesses will have similar P&L categories, such as **cost of goods sold** and rent. However, some industries will have unique expenses. For example, in our example below, MWI has a category titled *Widget Oil Expense*. Only widget manufacturers will have a widget oil expense category.

Cost of Goods Sold (def.)
The direct costs required to produce a product or service, such as materials and direct labor.

Sample Profit & Loss Statement

Sources of Revenue	FY-1	FY-2	FY-3
Widget Sales (Total Revenue)	$2,000,000	$2,487,500	$5,022,250
Cost of Goods Sold	– $400,000	– $500,000	– $1,250,000
Net Revenues	**$1,600,000**	**$1,987,500**	**$3,772,250**
Expenses	**FY-1**	**FY-2**	**FY-3**
Rents & Leases	$60,000	$72,000	$150,000
Telephones	$5,000	$6,000	$8,500
Utilities	$14,000	$17,000	$32,000
Payroll Expense	$1,148,000	$1,537,800	$1,994,080
Transportation & Shipping	$50,000	$70,000	$100,000
Business Insurance	$12,000	$15,000	$20,000
Computers	$12,000	$8,000	$48,000
Meals & Entertainment	$7,000	$8,500	$10,000
Travel	$14,000	$15,500	$18,000
Furniture, Fixtures & Equipment (FF&E)*	$56,000	$6,000	$18,000
Office Expense	$21,000	$32,000	$50,000
Office Supplies	$14,000	$15,000	$18,000
Widget Oil Expense	$2,000	$2,500	$3,000
Postage	$5,800	$7,400	$12,000
Total Expenses	$1,420,800	$1,812,700	$2,481,580
Profit / (Loss)	$179,200	$174,800	$1,290,670

Notes on the profit and loss statement:

- ** FF&E (FY-1) includes the cost of the new equipment of $49,849.51 and other FF&E expenses.*
- *Profits are lower in FY-1 and FY-2 as the company adds equipment and staff (expenses) to increase capacity for production of the X-Widget which goes on sale in FY-3.*

Ultimate BUSINESS PLANNING

For Visionary Start-Ups & Revolutionary Companies

My Company's 3-Year Profit and Loss Statement Worksheet

	Fiscal Year 1	Fiscal Year 2	Fiscal Year 3
Income			
Gross Receipts/Sales			
Less: Returns and Allowances			
Less: Cost of Goods Sold			
Gross Profit/(Loss)			
Expenses			
Advertising			
Car and truck expense			
Commissions and fees			
Contract labor			
Employee/fringe benefit programs			
Health insurance			
Business insurance			
Legal and professional services			
Office expense			
Pension/profit-sharing plans			
Office rent/lease			
Leasehold improvements			
Vehicle & equipment rent/lease			
Other business property rent/lease			
Repairs and maintenance			
Office supplies			
Taxes & licenses			
Travel			
Meals & entertainment			
Telephones & Internet			
Utilities			
Wages not included in COGS			
Dues & subscriptions			
Postage & shipping			
Other expense 1			
Other expense 2			
Total Expenses			
Net Profit/(Loss)			

*"Great things in business
are never done by one person.
They're done by a team of people."*
Steve Jobs

Ultimate BUSINESS PLANNING
For Visionary Start-Ups & Revolutionary Companies

Notes and Worksheet Page

Pro Forma Cash Flow Statement

The cash flow statement reports the movement of cash and cash-equivalents into and out of your business.

The cash flow statement includes an opening balance, which is the amount of money in a company's accounts at the beginning of an accounting period. The positive or negative balance at the end of an accounting period is the opening balance for the accounting period that follows.

In addition to the opening and ending balances, the cash flow statement consists of three main parts: *Operating Activities*, *Investing Activities* and *Financing Activities*.

OPERATING ACTIVITIES

Operating activities include cash receipts from selling goods or providing services, as well as income from items such as interest and dividends. Operating activities also include your cash payments such as inventory, payroll, taxes, interest, utilities, and rent. The net amount of cash used by operating activities is the key figure on a statement of cash flows.

Examples of cash out from operating activities include the purchase of materials or inventory, wages paid to employees and contractors, rent and overhead expenses.

INVESTING ACTIVITIES

Investing activities include transactions involving the purchase and sale of securities, land, buildings, equipment, and other assets not generally held for resale. It also includes making loans to individuals (owners or employees) or other businesses.

Examples of cash out from investing activities include the purchase of stock in another company or making a loan to an owner or employee.

FINANCING ACTIVITIES
Financing activities include transactions that involve receiving a loan or line of credit from a bank or investors.

Examples of cash out from financing activities include a monthly installment loan payment to a bank or investor.

"Rule No.1: Never lose money.
Rule No.2: Never forget rule No.1. "
Warren Buffett

Pro Forma Simplified Cash Flow Statement

The simplified cash flow statement format does not include detailed **CASH IN** and **CASH OUT** categories, but instead provides a summary of your company's cash flow projections. You can use a simplified cash flow statement in the body of your ultimate business plan or if you choose to include a cash flow statement in your executive summary, but you should include a detailed cash flow statement in the financial plan section of your ultimate business plan.

Use the worksheet on the next page to create a simplified monthly cash flow statement for FY-1.

Sample Simplified Quarterly Cash Flow Statement

CASH IN	FY-1	FY-2	FY-3
Opening/Beginning Cash Balance	$275,000	$519,200	$369,000
Cash In from Operating Activities	$2,000,000	$2,487,500	$5,022,250
Cash In from Investing Activities	$50,000	($15,000)	$10,000
Cash In from Financing Activities	$100,000	$0	$0
Total Cash Available for Operations	$2,425,000	$2,991,700	$5,401,250
CASH OUT			
Cash Out from Operating Activities	$1,820,800	$2,312,700	$3,731,580
Cash Out from Investing Activities	$75,000	$300,000	$500,000
Cash Out from Financing Activities	$10,000	$10,000	$22,850
Total Cash Out	$1,905,800	$2,622,700	$4,254,430
CASH FLOW	$519,200	$369,000	$1,146,820

Ultimate **BUSINESS PLANNING**

For Visionary Start-Ups & Revolutionary Companies

My Company's Simplified Monthly Cash Flow Statement for FY-1

SIMPLIFIED CASH FLOWS	Q1			Q2			Q3			Q4		
	Month 1	Month 2	Month 3	Month 4	Month 5	Month 6	Month 7	Month 8	Month 9	Month 10	Month 11	Month 12
Opening/Beginning Cash Balance												
Cash In from Operating Activities												
Cash In from Investing Activities												
Cash In from Financing Activities												
Total Cash Available for Operations												
CASH OUT												
Cash Out from Operating Activities												
Cash Out from Investing Activities												
Cash Out from Financing Activities												
Total Cash Out												
CASH FLOW												

Pro Forma Detailed Cash Flow Statement

To help you prepare a detailed cash flow statement, some common **CASH IN** and **CASH OUT** categories have been provided below. If you know of any business- or industry-specific categories not listed below but that are related to your company, make sure to include them in your pro forma quarterly cash flow statements.

Common CASH IN Categories
Cash sales
Returns and allowances
Collections on accounts receivable
Interest, other income
Loan proceeds
Owner contributions

Common CASH OUT Categories		
Advertising	Pension and profit-sharing plan	Wages (less emp. credits)
Commissions and fees	Purchases for resale	Loan principal payment
Contract labor	Office/Facility: Rent or lease	Capital purchases
Employee benefit programs	Rent or lease: equipment	To reserve and/or escrow
Insurance (other than health)	Rent or lease: vehicles	Other interest expense
Interest expense	Repairs and maintenance	Other startup costs
Materials and supplies (in COGS)	Supplies (not in COGS)	Owner's withdrawal
Meals and entertainment	Taxes and licenses	Miscellaneous/Other
Mortgage interest	Travel	
Office expense	Utilities	

*Tip! Perform an internet search for **"how to prepare business plan financials"**
for additional assistance on preparing this or any other business plan financial statement.*

Ultimate BUSINESS PLANNING
For Visionary Start-Ups & Revolutionary Companies

My Company's Detailed Quarterly Cash Flow Statement for FYs 1-3

ACCOUNTING PERIOD	FY-1	FY-2	FY-3
Opening/Beginning Balance			
CASH IN			
Cash sales			
Returns and allowances			
Collections on accounts receivable			
Interest, other income			
Loan proceeds			
Owner contributions			
TOTAL CASH RECEIPTS			
TOTAL CASH AVAILABLE FOR OPERATIONS			
CASH OUT			
Advertising			
Commissions and fees			
Contract labor			
Employee benefit programs			
Insurance (other than health)			
Interest expense			
Materials and supplies (in COGS)			
Meals and entertainment			
Mortgage interest			
Office expense			
Other interest expense			
Pension and profit-sharing plan			
Purchases for resale			
Rent or lease			
Rent or lease: vehicles, equipment			
Repairs and maintenance			
Supplies (not in COGS)			
Taxes and licenses			
Travel			
Utilities			
Wages (less emp. credits)			
Miscellaneous			
Loan principal payment			
Capital purchases			
Other startup costs			
To reserve and/or escrow			
Owners' withdrawal			
TOTAL CASH PAID OUT			
CASH ON HAND (End of the Month)			

*"There are many pathways to success,
but only one beginning...
An idea backed by a burning desire to achieve it."*
Norman David Roussell

Ultimate **BUSINESS PLANNING**

For Visionary Start-Ups & Revolutionary Companies

Notes and Worksheet Page

Ultimate **BUSINESS PLANNING**
For Visionary Start-Ups & Revolutionary Companies

Pro Forma Balance Sheet

The balance sheet is a snap shot of your company's financial position at a specific point in time.

For example, a balance sheet dated December 31st, 2020, shows the point in time when all transactions for the 2020 fiscal year have been recorded. The balance sheet is also known as a *Statement of Financial Position.*

The balance sheet is important to bankers and investors because it reveals the company's **assets**, **liabilities** and **owner's equity**. If a company's balance sheet has too much debt, or too few assets, it may be difficult to secure a bank loan or line of credit.

Assets (def.)	*Liabilities (def.)*
Everything the company owns that can be converted into cash.	*Includes all the debts the company owes to creditors.*

BALANCE SHEET FORMULA

ASSETS = LIABILITIES
+
OWNER'S
EQUITY

Owner's Equity (def.)
Mathematically, Total Assets minus Total Liabilities. Also known as Net Assets, Net Worth or Shareholder's Equity.

Assets include:
- Current assets include cash and other assets that can be converted into cash quickly, such as certificates of deposit, savings and accounts receivable.
- Long-term or fixed assets included land, buildings and equipment that takes longer than a year to convert into cash.

Liabilities include:
- Current liabilities include debts that must be repaid within a year such as accounts payable and the current portion of long-term debts (less than 12-months).
- Long-term liabilities include debts that come due and payable in more than one year, such as mortgages, loans, bonds payable, capital leases and pension liabilities.

Owner's Equity includes:
- **Paid-in capital-** The amount invested in the company at start-up by owners or that the company received when it issued membership shares (in an LLC) or capital stock (in a corporation) to investors.
- **Retained earnings-** The cumulative earnings of the company that are invested back into the company, minus cumulative dividends paid-out to investors.
- **Treasury stock-** The amounts spent by the company to repurchase, but not retire, membership shares or capital stock.

Ultimate BUSINESS PLANNING
For Visionary Start-Ups & Revolutionary Companies

Sample Balance Sheet

Assets		Liabilities	
Current Assets		**Current Liabilities**	
Cash	$300,000	Accounts Payable	$90,000
Savings	$50,000	Current Portion of Long-Term Debt	$10,000
Certificates of Deposit	$100,000	Short-Term Notes Payable	$50,000
Accounts Receivable	$175,000	-----	$0
Inventory	$125,000	-----	$0
Total Current Assets	**$750,000**	**Total Current Liabilities**	**$150,000**
Long-Term Assets		**Long-Term Liabilities**	
Machinery & Equipment	$500,000	Mortgages Payable	$510,000
Land & Buildings	$850,000	Loans Payable	$90,000
Total Long-Term Assets	**$1,350,000**	**Total Long-Term Liabilities**	**$600,000**
		Total Liabilities	**$750,000**
		Owner's Equity*	
		Paid-In Capital	$220,000
		Retained Earnings	$700,000
		Treasury Stock	$400,000
		Total Owner's Equity	**$1,350,000**
Total Assets	**$2,100,000**	**Total Liabilities & Owner's Equity**	**$2,100,000**

* Owner's Equity is also known as Shareholder's, Stockholder's or Member's Equity depending on the type of company. **Plural:** *Owners', Shareholders', Stockholders' or Members'.*

VERTICAL BALANCE SHEET FORMAT

ASSETS

- Current Assets
- Long-Term/Fixed Assets

TOTAL ASSETS

LIABILITIES

- Current Liabilities
- Long-Term Liabilities
- **TOTAL LIABILITIES**

SHAREHOLDERS' EQUITY

- Paid-In Capital
- Retained Earnings
- Treasury Stock

TOTAL SHAREHOLDERS' EQUITY

TOTAL LIABILITIES & SHAREHOLDERS' EQUITY

A vertical balance sheet presents the balance sheet in a single column, with asset line items, followed by liability line items, and ending with shareholders' equity line items. Within each category, line items are presented in decreasing order of liquidity.

The vertical format is typically used to present financial statement information in a side-by-side format allowing for a year-to-year comparison of categories.

The vertical format is also used for other financial statements, including the cash flow statement and income statement.

Ultimate **BUSINESS PLANNING**

For Visionary Start-Ups & Revolutionary Companies

My Company's 3-Year Balance Sheet

	Fiscal Year 1	Fiscal Year 2	Fiscal Year 3
Current Assets			
Total Current Assets			

Fixed Assets			
Total Fixed Assets			

Total Assets			

Current Liabilities			
Total Current Liabilities			

Long-Term Liabilities			
Total Long-Term Liabilities			

Shareholders' Equity			
Paid In Capital			
Retained Earnings			
Treasury Stock			
Total Shareholders' Equity			

Total Liabilities & Shareholders' Equity			

*"Great companies are
built on great products."*
Elon Musk

Ultimate BUSINESS PLANNING
For Visionary Start-Ups & Revolutionary Companies

Pro Forma Ratio Analysis

Bankers and investors use ratio analysis to evaluate a company's overall financial and operating performance in key areas- Liquidity, profitability, efficiency and solvency.

Ratio analysis is used to:

- Compare companies of similar size;
- Compare companies within the same industry;
- Compare a company's performance between different time periods; and
- Compare a single company to industry averages.

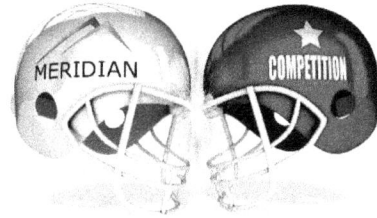

Some of the key financial ratios used in business planning include:

- **Liquidity Ratios**, which measure the availability of cash to pay debts. Key liquidity ratios for business planning include:
    - Current Ratio
    - Quick Ratio

- **Profitability Ratios**, which measure the company's use of its assets, and control of its expenses. Key profitability ratios for business planning include:
    - Gross Margin Ratio
    - Profit Margin Ratio
    - Return on Assets

- **Efficiency Ratio**, also known as activity ratios, which measure how effective the company is at maximizing the use of its resources. Key efficiency ratios for business planning include:
    - Inventory Turnover Ratio

- **Solvency Ratios**, also known as debt ratios, which measure the company's ability to repay its long-term debts. Key solvency ratios for business planning include:
    - Debt Ratio
    - Debt to Equity Ratio

My Accounting Course
accounting education for the rest of us

The ratio definitions and formulas are from **www.myaccountingcourse.com**. *The website provides a wealth of information, including more financial ratios, guidance on preparing financial statements and easy-to-understand lessons on bookkeeping and accounting.*

RATIO & DEFINITION	FORMULA
CURRENT RATIO The current ratio is a liquidity and efficiency ratio that measures a firm's ability to pay off its short-term liabilities with its current assets. The current ratio is an important measure of liquidity because short-term liabilities are due within the next year. This means that a company has a limited amount of time in order to raise the funds to pay for these liabilities.	Current Assets ÷ Current Liabilities
QUICK RATIO The quick ratio or acid test ratio is a liquidity ratio that measures the ability of a company to pay its current liabilities when they come due with only quick assets. Quick assets are current assets that can be converted to cash within 90-days or in the short-term. Cash, cash equivalents, short-term investments or marketable securities and current accounts receivable are considered quick assets.	(Current Assets – Inventory) ÷ Current Liabilities
GROSS MARGIN RATIO Gross margin ratio is a profitability ratio that compares the gross margin of a business to the net sales. This ratio measures how profitable a company sells its inventory or merchandise. In other words, the gross profit ratio is essentially the percentage markup on merchandise from its cost. This is the pure profit from the sale of inventory that can go to paying operating expenses.	(Revenue – Cost of Goods Sold) ÷ Revenue
PROFIT MARGIN RATIO The profit margin ratio, also called the return on sales ratio or gross profit ratio, is a profitability ratio that measures the amount of net income earned with each dollar of sales generated by comparing the net income and net sales of a company. In other words, the profit margin ratio shows what percentage of sales are left over after all expenses are paid by the business. Creditors and investors use this ratio to measure how effectively a company can convert sales into net income.	Net Profit ÷ Revenue-Cost of Goods Sold)

Ultimate BUSINESS PLANNING
For Visionary Start-Ups & Revolutionary Companies

RATIO & DEFINITION	FORMULA
RETURN ON ASSETS The return on assets ratio is a profitability ratio that measures the net income produced by total assets during a period by comparing net income to the average total assets. In other words, the return on assets ratio or ROA measures how efficiently a company can manage its assets to produce profits during a period. The ratio helps both management and investors see how well the company can convert its investment in assets into profits.	Net Income ÷ Total Assets
INVENTORY TURNOVER RATIO The inventory turnover ratio is an efficiency ratio that shows how effectively inventory is managed by comparing cost of goods sold with average inventory for a period. This measures how many times average inventory is sold during a period. Inventory turnover is a measure of how efficiently a company can control its merchandise, so it is important to have a high turn. This shows the company does not overspend by buying too much inventory and wastes resources by storing non-salable inventory. Average Inventory = (Beginning Inventory + Ending Inventory) ÷ 2	Cost of Goods Sold ÷ Average Inventory
DEBT RATIO Debt ratio is a solvency ratio that measures a firm's total liabilities as a percentage of its total assets. In a sense, the debt ratio shows a company's ability to pay off its liabilities with its assets. Companies with higher levels of liabilities compared with assets are considered highly leveraged and more risky for lenders.	Total Liabilities ÷ Total Assets
DEBT TO EQUITY RATIO The debt to equity ratio is a financial, liquidity ratio that compares a company's total debt to total equity. The debt to equity ratio shows percentage of financing the company receives from creditors and investors. A high debt to equity ratio shows that a company has taken out many more loans and has had contributions by shareholders or owners. A lower debt to equity ratio usually implies a more stable business with the potential of longevity.	Total Liabilities ÷ Total Equity

Ultimate BUSINESS PLANNING
For Visionary Start-Ups & Revolutionary Companies

Sample Ratio Analysis

The ratio analysis is based on MWI's *Sample Pro Forma Profit and Loss Statement* on page 101 and *Sample Pro Forma Balance Sheet* on page 114.

RATIO/FORMULA	CALCULATION	RESULT	GOOD
CURRENT RATIO Current Assets ÷ Current Liabilities	$750,000 ÷ $150,000	5.0	MWI can pay off all current liabilities 5.0 times with current assets.
QUICK RATIO (Current Assets-Inventory) ÷ Current Liabilities	($750,000-$125,000) ÷ $150,000	4.17	MWI can pay off all current liabilities 4.17 times with quick assets and still have inventory left over.
GROSS MARGIN RATIO (Revenue-Cost of Goods Sold) ÷ Revenue	$2,000,000-$400,000) ÷ $2,000,000	80%	MWI has a high gross margin ratio so the company will have enough money (80%) to pay operating expenses.
PROFIT MARGIN RATIO Net Profit ÷ (Revenue-Cost of Goods Sold)	$179,000 ÷ ($2,000,000-$400,000)	11.9%	MWI converted 11.9% of sales into profits.
RETURN ON ASSETS Net Income ÷ Total Assets	$179,000 ÷ $2,100,000	8.5%	Every dollar that MWI invested in assets during the year produced $.085 of net income.
INVENTORY TURNOVER RATIO Cost of Goods Sold ÷ Average Inventory*	$400,000 ÷ [($0.00+$125,000)/2]	1.6	MWI sold its average inventory slightly more than 1½ times during the year.
DEBT RATIO Total Liabilities ÷ Total Assets	$750,000 ÷ $2,100,000	35.7%	MWI has over 3 times as many assets as liabilities, a relatively low debt ratio.
DEBT TO EQUITY RATIO Total Liabilities ÷ Total Equity	$750,000 ÷ $1,350,000	55.6%	MWI has slightly more than half as many liabilities than there is equity, meaning company assets are funded almost 2-to-1 by investors versus creditors.

***Inventory Turnover Formula**: Since, in our example, it is FY-1 for MWI, beginning inventory is $0.00. Therefore, the **average inventory** is calculated as ($0.00+$125,000) ÷ 2.*

SUPPORTTING DOCUMENTS

The list below is an example of the typical supporting documents required by bankers and investors to accompany a business plan. More or fewer documents may be required, depending on the source and type of financing you are seeking.

- Completed bank or lender application
- One-page loan proposal (Page 129)
- Articles of Incorporation or Articles of Organization
- Tradename or "Doing Business As" registration
- Corporate Bylaws or limited liability company Operating Agreement
- City, state and local business licenses
- Industry-specific business and trade licenses
- Federal Employer Identification Number (EIN)
- State and local tax ID numbers
- Tri-bureau credit reports on each owner (< 30 days old)
- Personal new worth statement for each owner (< 30 days old)
- Personal tax returns with all schedules for each owner (Past 3 years)
- Sources and amounts of the capital contributed by owners to start or grow the business
- Résumés of owners, key employees, board members and consultants
- Job descriptions for all positions in the company
- Pro forma profit and loss statement, cash flow statement and balance sheet (FYs 1-3)
- Profit and loss statements, cash flow statements and balance sheet for the past 3 years (Existing businesses only)
- Business income tax reports (Past 3 years)
- Schedule of all business debts (Notes and accounts payable, contracts, leases payable, etc.)
- Aged accounts payable and receivable reports
- Schedule of fixed assets to be acquired with a loan or investment
- Appraisal on real estate to be acquired with a loan or investment (< 90 days old)
- Copies of existing contracts with clients, office leases, franchise agreements, purchase or buy-sell agreements and partnership agreements
- Copies of all company insurance policies:
    - General liability, workmen's compensation and/or errors and omission
    - Employee benefits (For example, health, disability and profit sharing)
    - Key employee
    - Surety bonding
    - Fidelity bonding

Ultimate BUSINESS PLANNING
For Visionary Start-Ups & Revolutionary Companies

Use the business plan checklist to ensure your ultimate business plan contains all the elements required by bankers and investors.

Section of the Business Plan	Component of the Business Plan	Included? Yes | No| N/A
Front Matter	Cover	
	Table of Contents	
	Cover Letter	
	Confidentiality Agreement	
Executive Summary	Company Background	
	Products and Services	
	Mission Statement	
	Vision Statement	
	Values Statement	
	Objectives	
	Start-Up Costs Table	
	Pro Forma Sales Graph	
	Keys to Success	
Management Plan	Management Plan Summary	
	Company Ownership	
	Key Personnel	
	Consultants (Master Mind Group)	
	Personnel Plan and Table	
	Employee Benefit Plans	
	SWOT Analysis	
	Milestones	
	Exit Strategy	
Products and Services	Products and Services Summary	
	Features and Benefits of the Products and Services	
	Patents, Trademarks and Copyrights	
	Licensing and Franchise Agreements	
	Future Products and Services	
Marketing Plan	Marketing Plan Summary	
	Market Segmentation Analysis	
	Target Market Analysis	
	Market Trend Analysis	
	Marketing Strategy	

Ultimate BUSINESS PLANNING

For Visionary Start-Ups & Revolutionary Companies

Business plan checklist (continued)

Section of the Business Plan	Component of the Business Plan	Included? Yes | No| N/A
Website and Social Media Plans	Website Development Plan	
	Website Marketing Strategy	
	Social Media Development Plan	
	Social Media Marketing Strategy	

Section of the Business Plan	Component of the Business Plan	Included? Yes | No| N/A
Sales Plan	Sales Plan Summary	
	Sales Plan Table (By Units)	
	Sales Plan Table (Revenue)	

Section of the Business Plan	Component of the Business Plan	Included? Yes | No| N/A
Financial Plan	Financial Plan Summary	
	Start-Up (Expansion) Cost Summary and Table	
	Break-Even Point Analysis	
	Pro Forma Sales Forecast	
	Pro Forma Income Statement	
	Pro Forma Cash Flow Statement	
	Pro Forma Cash Flow Statement	
	Pro Forma Balance Sheet	
	Ratio Analysis	

Supporting Documents

*"Mistakes are always forgivable,
if one has the courage to admit them."*
Bruce Lee

Ultimate BUSINESS PLANNING

For Visionary Start-Ups & Revolutionary Companies

EVALUATING YOUR BUSINESS PLAN

Use the *Business Plan Evaluator* to assess the quality of your ultimate business plan. Your evaluation should be honest and unbiased. If you are unable to evaluate your business plan objectively, ask a member of your team or master mind group to evaluate your business plan on the flowing criteria:

Criteria	Points
The business plan does an **excellent** job	5
The business plan does a **very good** job	4
The business plan does a **good** job	3
The business plan does a **fair** job	2
The business plan does a **poor** job	1

EVALUATION CRITERIA	SCORE
1. The executive summary can stand alone as a clear, concise and compelling overview of the entire business plan.	
2. The executive summary entices the reader to review the entire business plan.	
3. The business plan presents a clear mission and vision for the company.	
4. The business plan shows that the owners, managers and consultants have the skills and experience to successfully start, manage and grow the company.	
5. The business plan shows the owners have made a personal investment of capital, credit, equipment or other tangible assets to start and grow the company.	
6. The business plan clearly defines the features and benefits of the company's products and services and why potential customers should buy them.	
7. The business plan has a well-defined target market for the company's products and services that is large enough to support the sales projections.	
8. The business plan has realistic and achievable short-term, mid-term and long-term objectives.	
9. The business plan presents realistic financial projections and not "pie in the sky" projections that will not pass the test with bankers or investors.	
10. The business plan identifies clear and workable strategies to start and grow the company from day one.	
TOTAL EVALUATION SCORE	

Ultimate **BUSINESS PLANNING**

For Visionary Start-Ups & Revolutionary Companies

Business Plan Evaluator Scoring System

If...		Then...
Your score is	**≤20**	The plan should be totally revised. Rewrite the plan and evaluate the plan again. If the score does not improve significantly after the rewrite, you might want to consider changing your business model or abandoning the business plan altogether.
Your score is	**21-30**	The idea or business model might be good, but the plan will need some work before it qualifies for funding.
Your score is	**31-41**	Your plan is very good, but it needs to be spruced-up. Tip! Add more charts and images to make the plan a little more interesting for the reader.
Your score is	**42-50**	Your plan is ready to be presented to bankers and investors for funding. Good luck!

GETTING YOUR BUSINESS FUNDED

Why is it difficult for small businesses to obtain a business loan from a bank[6]?

Funding Facts:

- About 33% of businesses fail within the first 2 years in business;
- About 50% of all businesses survive only 5 years;
- About 33% of all businesses survive 10 years; and
- 82% of all businesses fail because of cash flow problems.

The U.S. Small Business Administration's (SBA) published statistics from 2015, breaking down the approval rates along gender, ethnicity and location lines with the following revelations:

- There was a 29% approval rate for minority-owned businesses versus 57% for white-owned;
- There was a 71% approval rate for male-owned businesses versus 29% for female-owned;
- There was a 67% approval rate for existing businesses versus 33% for new business; and
- There was a 17% approval for rural companies versus 83% for urban.

Biz2Credit's *Small Business Lending Index* reported that in March 2016:

- Big banks approved 23% of funding requests;
- Institutional lenders[7] approved 62.8% of funding requests;
- Small banks approved 48.7% of funding requests;
- Alternative lenders approved 60.7% of funding requests; and
- Credit unions approved 42% of funding requests.

Banks view most start-ups and small businesses as high risk. Banks prefer to loan money to businesses with a track record of revenue growth and positive cash flow. If a business has yet to prove that it is financially sound, it will be difficult to secure funding.

While statistics prove it is more difficult to get a loan as a minority or woman or restaurant or rural business, you can give your business a better chance of getting funded by remembering these tips:

1. A sensible business purpose must always accompany a loan request;
2. Know the lending criteria of potential funding sources before you apply for a loan;
3. Know your personal credit scores and business credit scores, and be prepared to explain all potentially negative items before you apply for a loan;
4. Know what your request needs to have in it and what it does not; and
5. Apply for funding before, not after, your business needs money.

---

[6] Source: www.Fundera.com
[7] Savings Banks and Life Insurance Companies

Crowdfunding

Crowdfunding is the process of raising money to fund what is typically a project or business venture through many donors using an online platform. The fundraising window is usually finite - 90 days, for instance - and the fees and rules vary across platforms[8].

Crowdfunding allows entrepreneurs to reach a much greater pool of potential investors while generating interest and, hopefully, validating the potential market for a product or service.

Below is a list of three of the top crowdfunding websites.

Gofundme.com   Indiegogo.com   Kickstarter.com

Visit **www.crowdfunding.com** to learn more about crowdfunding as a source of capital and for a list of the top crowdfunding websites.

---

[8] Source: www.entrepreneur.com

Ultimate **BUSINESS PLANNING**
For Visionary Start-Ups & Revolutionary Companies

THE ONE-PAGE LOAN PROPOSAL

In addition to preparing a business plan and completing a loan application, you should also summarize your loan in the form of a *One-Page Loan Proposal*. The *One-Page Loan Proposal* includes, at a minimum, the following information:

1. Date of the proposal
2. Borrower(s)
3. Loan amount you are seeking
4. Uses of the funds
5. Type of loan
6. Proposed interest rate
7. Proposed term of the loan
8. Loan closing date
9. Loan repayment begins
10. Loan repayment ends
11. Fees
12. Collateral
13. Guarantees
14. Source of loan repayment

Meridian Widgets, Inc.
Loan Proposal

Purpose of the Loan

The $1000,000.00 loan proceeds will be used to purchase equipment, expansion expenses and working capital. The owner is investing $20,000.00 cash into the business. Additional assets may be pledged as collateral. Details of the loan proposal are below.

Date of proposal	February 1, 20XX
Borrower	John Doe, Owner/CEO- MWI, Inc.
Amount	$100,000.00
Use of proceeds	Equipment and working capital
Type of loan	Fixed term loan
Interest rate	7.0% (preferred); maximum 8.5%
Term	7 years (84 months)
Closing date	February 20, 20XX
Repayment begins	Thirty (30) days after closing or receipt of funds
Repayment ends	February 20XX (7 years)
Fees	As required by lender
Collateral	Accounts receivable, inventory, equipment and real estate
Guarantee	Business; Personal (If required)
Source(s) of loan repayment	Cash flow from operations

Ultimate BUSINESS PLANNING
For Visionary Start-Ups & Revolutionary Companies

My Company's One-Page Loan Proposal Worksheet

Date of Proposal	
Borrower(s)	
Loan amount	
Use of proceeds	
Type of funding	
Preferred/maximum interest rate	
Term	
Closing date	
Repayment begins	
Repayment ends	
Fees	
Collateral	
Guarantees	
Source(s) of funds for loan repayment	

"The price of success is hard work, dedication to the job at hand, and the determination that whether we win or lose, we have applied the best of ourselves to the task at hand."

Vince Lombardi

Notes and Worksheet Page

Ultimate **BUSINESS PLANNING**
For Visionary Start-Ups & Revolutionary Companies

SMALL BUSINESS RESOURCES FOR SUCCESS

You are not alone! Take advantage of some of the free and low-cost resources available to America's entrepreneurs.

www.sba.gov
The U.S. Small Business Administration (SBA) is an independent Federal government agency created to aid, counsel, assist and protect the interests of small business concerns through access to capital, entrepreneurial development, government contracting and small business advocacy.

www.score.org
SCORE is a nonprofit organization with over 13,000 volunteers who help small businesses start, grow and succeed nationwide by providing confidential business counseling to entrepreneurs at no charge.

www.americassbdc.org
The Association of Small Business Development Centers has over 1,000 service centers throughout the U.S., Guam, American Samoa, Puerto Rico and the U.S. Virgin Islands that provide no-cost business consulting and low-cost training for America's small businesses.

www.mbda.gov
The Minority Business Development Agency (MBDA), a part of the U.S. Department of Commerce, is an entrepreneurially-focused Federal agency with a mission to actively promote the growth and competitiveness of large, medium and small minority business enterprises (MBEs) in the U.S.

www.hud.gov
The purpose of *HUD's Small Business Resource Guide* is to provide a compendium of practical information on national, state and local small business resources which assist individuals who are about to start or expand a business. In addition to providing basic information on existing small businesses programs and contracting with the Federal government, there is specific guidance on contracting with the Department of Housing and Urban Development (HUD) and the contracting opportunities available with HUD grantees.

www.trade.gov
The U.S. Commercial Service is the trade promotion arm of the U.S. Department of Commerce's International Trade Administration. U.S. Commercial Service trade professionals in over 100 U.S. cities and in more than 75 countries help U.S. companies get started in exporting or increase sales to new global markets.

www.sba.gov (Search: Women's Business Centers)
The U.S. Small Business Administration's Women's Business Center Program consists of Women's Business Resource Centers in the U.S. and Puerto Rico that provide business training, counseling and resources to help women and men start and grow successful businesses.

www.vetbiz.gov

The U.S. Department of Veteran Affair's website dedicated to helping veterans of the armed forces start and grow successful businesses.

www.annualcreditreport.com

This central Federal government website allows you to request a free personal credit file disclosure, commonly called a credit report, once every 12 months from each of the nationwide consumer credit reporting companies: Equifax, Experian and TransUnion.

www.dnb.com

Dun & Bradstreet (DNB) is the world's leading provider of business credit reports and the business credit bureau that can assist you in establishing a business credit profile.

A DNB DUNS Number is required to do business with the U.S. Federal government. The DUNS Number is free.

www.export.gov

Export.gov helps businesses plan their international sales strategies and overcome challenges of global market access and trade compliance.

www.gsa.gov

The General Services Administration (GSA) is the purchasing agent for the U.S. government that connects Federal buyers with commercial products and services.

www.census.gov

The U.S. Census Bureau's website provides up-to-date statistical data on the U.S. population, U.S. business and industry and the U.S. economy.

www.aptac-us.org

Operating through Procurement Technical Assistance Centers in the U.S., Guam and Puerto Rico, the Procurement Technical Assistance Program helps businesses compete for Federal, state and local government contracting opportunities by providing them with expert consulting services at little or no charge.

www.grants.gov

Grants.gov is the free central portal of the U.S. government where you can find and apply for all Federal grant opportunities.

www.ready.gov

Ready.gov helps individuals, families, and businesses prepare for and recover from natural and man-made disasters.

www.nist.gov (Search: Manufacturing Extension Partnership)

The National Institute of Standards and Technology's Hollings Manufacturing Extension Partnership (MEP) works with small and mid-sized U.S. manufacturers to help them create and retain jobs, increase profits and save time and money.

www.FBO.gov
"Fed Biz Opps" is the U.S. government's website where Federal contracting opportunities are posted.

www.usa.gov
USA.gov provides access to every Federal agency website as well as to state websites and local consumer and business resources.

www.sam.gov
Anyone seeking to do business with the Federal government must register with the System for Award Management (SAM). You must have a DUNS Number to register with SAM.

www.nwbc.gov
The National Women's Business Council is a bi-partisan Federal advisory council created to serve as an independent source of advice and counsel to the President, Congress, and the U.S. Small Business Administration on economic issues of importance to women business owners.

www.nmsdc.org
The National Minority Supplier Development Council certifies and matches minority owned businesses with over 3,600-member corporations that want to purchase goods and services.

www.associationexecs.com
Home of the National Trade and Associations Directory containing over 8,000 professional associations, professional societies and labor unions and their 35,000+ executives.

www.uschamber.com
The U.S. Chamber of Commerce is the world's largest business federation representing the interests of more than 3 million businesses of all sizes, sectors and regions.

- **www.uswcc.org**
  U.S. Women's Chamber of Commerce

- **www.nationalbcc.org**
  National Black Chamber of Commerce

- **www.uspaac.com**
  U.S. Pan Asian Chamber of Commerce

- **www.ushcc.org**
  U.S. Hispanic Chamber of Commerce

- **www.nglcc.org**
  National Gay & Lesbian Chamber of Commerce

www.businessdictionary.com
BusinessDictionary.com has over 20,000 definitions of business terms to help you gain a better understanding of key business terms, including the definitions used throughout this workbook.

Ultimate BUSINESS PLANNING
For Visionary Start-Ups & Revolutionary Companies

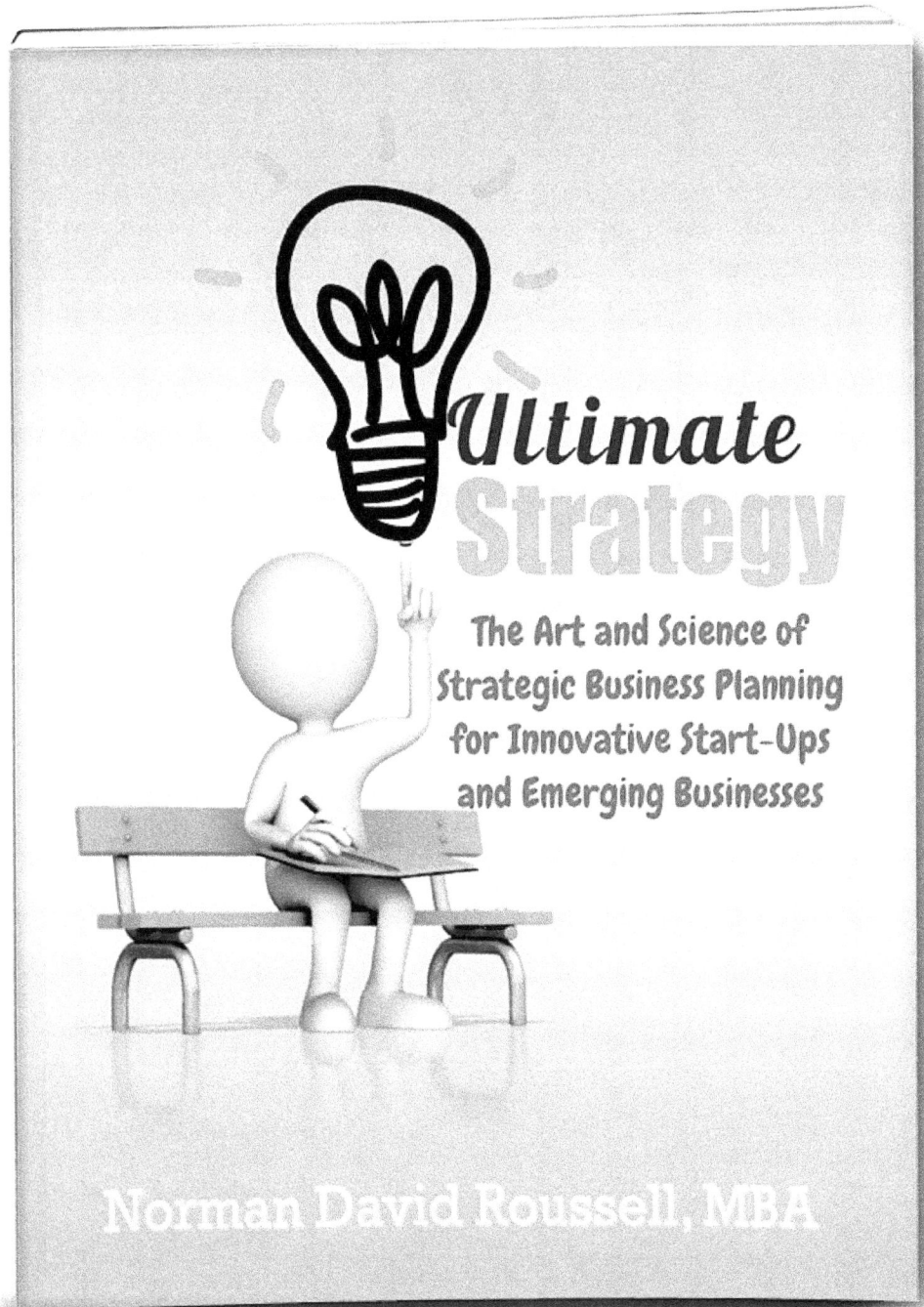

amazon.com

MERIDIAN

BUSINESS PLAN

John Doe, Founder & CEO
MERIDIAN WIDGETS, INC.
1234 Main Street
Springfield, USA

Phone (800) 555-1212
Fax (800) 555-1234

www.mwiwidgets.com

January 7, 2020

MERIDIAN

January 7, 2020

Dear Reader:

Thank you for taking time to review our company's business plan. I believe that you will see the great potential that we have in building a successful widget manufacturing and distribution company over the next three years.

My company is seeking a $100,000 loan to purchasing state-of-the-industry widget manufacturing equipment. With the equipment we will produce our new X-Widget, which will help MWI double revenues within three years. The increased capacity and new product will generate more than enough cash flow to repay the loan.

If you have any questions about our company or our business plan that you would like to discuss in person, I am available to meet at your convenience.

Again, thank you in advance for reviewing our business plan.

Sincerely yours,

John Doe

John Doe, Founder & CEO

MERIDIAN

CONFIDENTIALITY AGREEMENT

The reader of this business plan acknowledges that the information contained herein is personal and confidential and cannot be discussed, copied or disseminated without the prior written consent of the owner of Meridian Widgets, Inc., Mr. John Doe.

Business Plan Copy 1 of 10 delivered to Mr. John Q. Banker on 01/07/2020.

Acknowledgement of receipt by

John Q. Banker

John Q. Banker

Meridian Widgets, Inc.
BUSINESS PLAN

1.0. Executive Summary

1.1. Company Background Summary

Meridian Widgets, Inc., (MWI), was founded in 2005 by John Doe. Headquartered in New Orleans, Louisiana, MWI is a manufacturer and distributor or widgets for industrial, construction and consumer applications. MWI has manufacturing facilities in New Orleans, LA and Flint, MI, and wholesales widgets to home improvement and hardware stores throughout North America and directly to consumers online.

1.2. Products and Services Summary

MWI manufactures widgets for three segments of the widget market. Our Industrial Widgets are manufactured for use in industrial manufacturing facilities. Our Deluxe Widgets are manufactured for use in heavy and light commercial construction. Our Standard Widgets are manufactured for non-commercial consumer applications such as home improvement projects. Our innovative widget design and manufacturing processes make our widgets twice as durable as our nearest competitor and come with a lifetime guarantee.

1.3. Mission Statement

MWI is dedicated to manufacturing and distributing the highest quality widgets in North American through our commitment to providing exceptional workmanship, sales and service to our customers.

1.4. Vision Statement

MWI's vision is to be the #1 widget manufacturer in North America within the next five years.

1.5. Values Statement

MWI is committed to acting honestly and ethically in all our transactions and dealings. We are committed to treating our employees, clients, suppliers and investors fairly and respectfully and we are dedicated to acting responsibly in the communities in which we work.

We will engage in no transaction that does not benefit everyone involved.

1.6. Objectives

1. Increase our company's client base from 50 to 200 clients within the next 12-months.
2. Decrease overhead expenses 20% by the end of FY-2.
3. Increase sales from $2,000,000.00 to over $7,500,000.00 by the end of FY-3.

1.7. Start-Up Costs Summary and Table

MWI is investing $20,000.00 along with a bank loan of $100,000.00 to purchase state-of-the industry manufacturing equipment and software to begin production of our new X-Widget. The Expansion Cost table, below, details the sources and uses of funds and the resulting working capital balance.

SOURCES OF EXPANSION CAPITAL	AMOUNT
Owner's Investment	$20,000.00
Bank Loan	$100,000.00
Total Expansion Capital	**$120,000.00**
EXPANSION EXPENSES	
Computers and Software	$15,000.00
Website and Supplies	$5,000.00
Legal and Consulting Expenses	$10,000.00
Purchase New Widget Manufacturing Equipment	$49,849.51
Miscellaneous Expansion Expenses	$2,500.00
Total Expansion Expenses	**$82,349.51**
WORKING CAPITAL BALANCE	**$37,650.49**

1.8. Pro Forma Sales Graphs

Pro Forma Sales by Product for MWI FYs 1-3

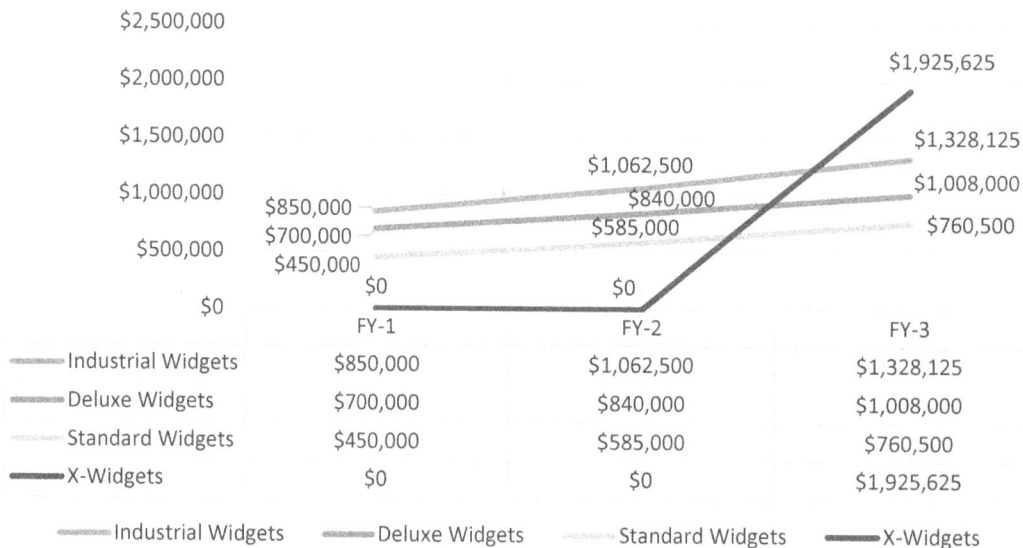

	FY-1	FY-2	FY-3
Industrial Widgets	$850,000	$1,062,500	$1,328,125
Deluxe Widgets	$700,000	$840,000	$1,008,000
Standard Widgets	$450,000	$585,000	$760,500
X-Widgets	$0	$0	$1,925,625

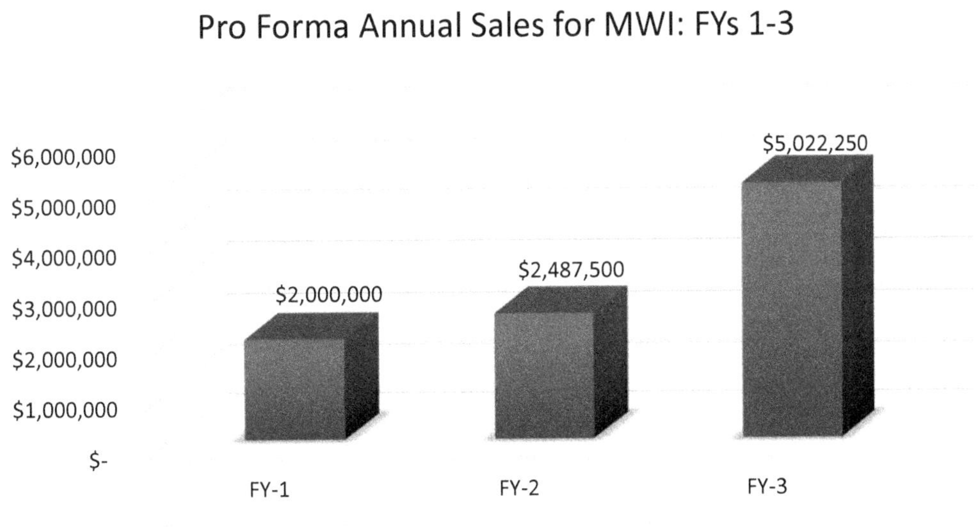
Pro Forma Annual Sales for MWI: FYs 1-3
$6,000,000
$5,000,000
$4,000,000
$3,000,000
$2,000,000
$1,000,000
$-
$2,000,000
$2,487,500
$5,022,250
FY-1
FY-2
FY-3

1.9. Keys to Success

1. To secure a minimum 7-year loan term on a bank loan.
2. Secure an interest rate at or below 10% on a bank loan.
3. Secure a patent on our new X-Widget by the end of FY-1.

2.0. Management Plan

2.1. Management Plan Summary

MWI, one of North America's leading widget manufacturing companies, is a Louisiana corporation founded in 2005 by John Doe. MWI is headquartered in New Orleans, LA, at 2600 London Ave., and maintains manufacturing facilities in New Orleans, LA, and Flint, MI. MWI has an exceptional team of owners, managers, staff and consultants and a highly qualified and engaged board of directors.

2.1.1. Company Ownership

John Doe is the CEO of MWI and owner of 90% of the company's outstanding shares. Jim Doe and Mary Doe own the remaining 10% of the company's shares.

2.1.2. Key Personnel

- Lexi Chan, Chief Operating Officer
- Malcolm Edward, Chief Technology Officer
- Zoey Marie, Chief Financial Officer

2.1.3. Board of Directors or Managers

- Dr. Dillard, President
- Mrs. J. Camille, Treasurer
- Mrs. M. Newman, Secretary
- Mr. S. Verrett, Board Member
- Mr. B. Gilmore, Board Member

2.1.4. Consultants

- E.H. Hampton, Management Consultant (Mentor)
- C. Blouin, CPA
- M. Cadet, Attorney
- E. Banquet, Business Banker
- T. Sandifer, Human Resources Conultant
- T. Greener, Insurance & Risk Management Consultant

2.2. Personnel Plan and Table

MWI has a workforce of 15 people, with a goal of staffing up to 24 by the beginning of FY-3 to oversee production of our new X-Widget. All of our manufacturing employees must be high school graduates and must complete a 4-month probationary period prior to being hired full time.

Simplified Personnel Plan Table

Management	6; 6; 6	$393,000	$432,400	$472,330	$1,297,730
Manufacturing	12; 17; 22	$763,000	$927,400	$1,367,7300	$1,760,400
TOTAL	**15; 17; 24**	**$1,148,000**	**$1,537,800**	**$1,994,080**	**$3,058,130**

2.3. Employee Benefit Plans

Every employee will be provided with health insurance and a term life insurance policy for $50,000 paid by the company. Employees will have an option to contribute to the company's 401(k) plan where the company will match contributions up to 10% of the employee's annual salary. If the company exceeds its annual sales goals by at least 20%, every employee will receive a bonus of up to 10% of his or her salary. We believe that our employee benefit plans offer competitive compensation and will allow MWI to attract and retain quality managers and employees.

2.4. SWOT Analysis

Strengths	**Weaknesses**
- Management team - Innovative products - Best warranty in the industry - Our team's combined experience	- Access to capital for expansion - Ineffective marketing plan - Inefficient distribution channels
Opportunities	**Threats**
- Growth of aerospace market - Licensing products to foreign manufacturers	- Rising cost of production - Chinese widget manufacturers

2.5. Milestones

MWI has identified several milestones to improve accountability and keep our team's expansion plan on track. Our milestones include:

Milestones Table

Task	Start Date	End Date	By
Write a business plan	01/07/20	02/20/20	Owner
Research lenders and apply for a loan	02/21/20	03/25/20	CFO
Secure a $100K loan or investment	03/26/20	06/18/20	Owner
Purchase and install the new widget equipment	07/01/20	07/11/20	COO
Train the staff to operate new widget equipment	07/11/20	11/15/20	Plant Manager
Begin producing X-Widgets	11/17/20	Ongoing Activity	Owners and staff

2.6. Exit Strategy

Once MWI achieves its vision of being the #1 widget company in North American, John Doe will begin to transfer 51% of the company's outstanding stock to his children and sell the remaining 39% of his shares in the company to the minority owners.

3.0. Products and Services

3.1. Products and Services Summary

MWI manufactures widgets for three segments of the widget market. Our Industrial Widgets are manufactured for use in industrial manufacturing facilities. Our Deluxe Widgets are manufactured for use in heavy and light commercial construction. Our Standard Widgets are manufactured for non-commercial consumer applications such as home improvement projects. *MWI is also developing the new X-Widget for use in the aerospace industry. The X-Widget will be the most advanced widget ever designed for aerospace applications and will help MWI double revenues by the end of FY-3.*

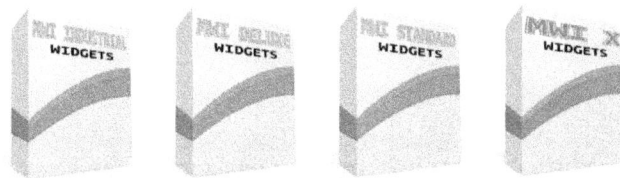

3.2. Features and Benefits of the Products and Services

MWI's 100% aluminum widgets weigh 40% less than traditional steel widgets. The lighter weight of MWI's aluminum widgets result in a 45% increase in performance and stability, allowing the company the ability to offer the only lifetime warranty in the widget industry.

3.3. Patents, Trademarks and Copyrights

MWI maintains patents for each of its widget designs and has applied for a provisional patent for our new X-Widget. MWI has a trademark for the company's logo and our CEO has published several trade publications for the widget industry, including the research paper, Widget Design Applications for the Aerospace Industry.

3.4. Licensing and Franchise Agreements

MWI does not have or offer any licensing or franchise agreements for its widget products. As we expand into the aerospace industry with our new X-Widget, we will consider offering licensing agreements to international widget manufacturers in South American and Europe.

3.5. Future Products and Services

MWI is in the final stages of development of the X-Widget. The X-Widget is designed for use in the aerospace industry and will be available for sale by the beginning of FY-3. MWI will concentrate efforts on launching the X-Widget and meeting the sales projections in this business plan before considering any other growth strategies.

4.0. Marketing Plan

4.1. Market Analysis Summary

The North American market for widgets has grown an average of 15% per year for the past five years because of new construction spending exceeding $700 billion annually in the U.S and $200 billion annually in Canada. Infrastructure spending in North American is projected to continue double digit growth for the next ten years, creating an ongoing demand for widgets.

The market for aerospace widgets is in its infancy because of new private space exploration companies. The new aerospace widget market is estimated at $50 billion annually. MWI will capitalize on the growing industry with the introduction of our patent-pending X-Widget by FY-3.

4.2. Market Segmentation Analysis

The market for widgets in North America is 20 million units annually and is divided into five main segments, with the largest segment being the standard widgets segment. MWI markets its widgets to the three largest segments of the widget market and plans to expand to the fourth largest segment, the aerospace widget market, by FY-3.

North American Widget Market Segmentation

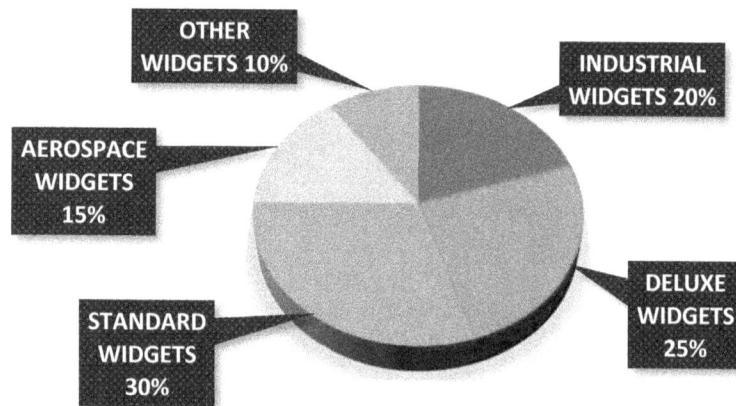

OTHER WIDGETS 10%

INDUSTRIAL WIDGETS 20%

AEROSPACE WIDGETS 15%

DELUXE WIDGETS 25%

STANDARD WIDGETS 30%

4.3. Target Market Analysis

MWI began by fabricating custom widgets for the commercial construction industry. Within two years, management had learned more about the market for widgets and set in motion a plan to manufacture widgets for the largest segments of the widget market to maximize the opportunity for long-term growth. As a result, MWI expanded into the manufacture of our brand of industrial widgets, deluxe widgets and standard widgets.

- For the industrial widget segment of the market, MWI will focus marketing efforts on specific companies with specific needs and opportunities. Customization is the value proposition we will offer this segment of the market. Based on our research, we expect the market for industrial widgets to grow at 15% per year over the next three years.

- For the deluxe widget segment of the market, MWI will focus marketing efforts on commercial construction and heavy construction customers. Durability, quality and a product warranty are the value propositions we will offer this segment of the market. Based on our research, we expect the market for deluxe widgets to grow at 20% per year over the next three years.

- For the standard widget market, MWI will focus marketing efforts on customers seeking widgets for a variety of non-commercial consumer applications. Variety and low cost are the value propositions we will offer this segment of the market. Based on our research, we expect the market for standard widgets to grow at 10% per year over the next three years.

4.4. Market Trend Analysis

Advances in manufacturing, technology and design have created new opportunities for widget applications in the aerospace industry. The emerging aerospace market is estimated at $50 billion annually, with growth rates projected up to 25% a year for the next ten years. MWI will take advantage of the aerospace industry opportunity with the introduction of the company's X-Widget. As trends in the widget industry continue to shift away from a 45% dependence on the construction industry, MWI's research team will continue to be an industry leader in developing and supplying widgets for new and emerging markets.

4.5. Marketing Strategy

MWI's marketing strategy will focus on improving brand awareness through a combination of paid radio, TV and print advertising and free social media marketing and publicity. We will budget at least $300,000 over the next 18-months towards implementing our marketing strategy. Each of our target market segments will be aligned with an effective combination of advertising and publicity to support our sales team. While each target market will require a unique marketing strategy, each will be designed to maximize the sales, market share and profit targets we have established in this business plan. MWI's management team recognizes the limitations of our experience, therefore we will hire a marketing consultant or firm to design and execute our marketing plans.

MWI's proposed marketing budget through the end of FY-3.

Marketing Budget Item	Estimated Cost
Marketing consultant/firm	$70,000
TV advertising campaigns	$110,000
Radio advertising campaigns	$40,000
Internet advertising campaigns	$30,000
Social media marketing campaigns	$20,000
Sponsorships and other campaigns	$30,000
TOTAL	**$300,000**

5.0. Website and Social Media Plans

5.1. Website Development Plan

MWI's website will included the following pages:

- **Home Page:** Includes information about our company's background;
- **Products Page:** Includes information and pictures of our industrial, deluxe and standard widgets, as well as information on our upcoming X-Widget;
- **E-Commerce Store:** Includes our widget products for sale online; and
- **Contact Us:** Allows customers and potential customers to contact call us or send us an e-mail with any questions or comments.

MWI will hire a consultant to build our new website and to ensure the site appears in the top search results for widgets by increasing the site's visibility in search engines, known as search engine optimization.

5.2. Social Media Development Plan

MWI will engage potential clients via social media by employing the following social media strategies:

- Daily Twitter posts about our widgets and how they are used by our clients;
- Weekly Facebook posts on trends in the widget industry; and
- Monthly YouTube video posts about how to use our widgets.

6.0. Sales Plan

6.1. Sales Plan Summary

MWI's sales success depends on our exceptional sales team's deep expertise in selling customers on the features and benefits of MWI widgets. MWI's strategy to demonstrate real world applications for our widgets will help us continue to have an industry-leading client closing rate of 80% and easily achieve both our unit sales and gross revenue sales targets during FYs 1-3. Furthermore, the company's $300,000.00 investment in marketing will provide the support necessary to achieve and likely exceed the sales targets in this business plan.

6.2. Sales Plan Table (Units)

Product	Unit Sales FY-1	Unit Sales FY-2	Unit Sales FY-3	Total
Industrial Widgets	100,000	125,000 (+25%)	156,250 (+25%)	381,250
Deluxe Widgets	200,000	240,000 (+20%)	288,000 (+20%)	728,000
Standard Widgets	250,000	325,000 (+30%)	422,500 (+30%)	997,500
X-Widgets	----	----	32,500 (New)	32,500
Total	**550,000**	**690,000 (≈25%)**	**900,000**	**2,140,000**

6.3. Sales Plan Table (Revenue)

Product	Selling Price	Revenue FY-1	Revenue FY-2	Revenue FY-3	Total Revenue FYs 1-3
Industrial Widgets	$8.50	$850,000	$1,062,500	$1,328,125	$3,240,625
Deluxe Widgets	$3.50	$700,000	$840,000	$1,008,000	$2,548,000
Standard Widgets	$1.80	$450,000	$585,000	$760,500	$1,795,000
X-Widgets	$59.25	$0	$0	$1,925,625	$1,925,625
Total		**$2,000,000**	**$2,487,500**	**$5,022,250**	**$9,509,750**

7.0. Financial Plan

7.1. Financial Plan Summary

MWI is seeking a $100,000.00 bank loan to purchase the equipment required to manufacture the new X-Widget. With the investment, MWI will be able to more than double sales from $2 million in FY-1 to over $5 million by the end of FY-3.

Our general assumptions include:

- Bank loan interest rate of 8%;
- Bank loan term of 7 years (85 months);
- Overhead will remain level at 15% per year; and
- Our business tax rate will be 35%.

Our comprehensive financial plan includes:

- Expansion Cost Table;
- Break-Even Point Analysis;
- Pro Forma Sales Forecast;
- Pro Forma Profit and Loss Statement;
- Pro Forma Profit and Loss Statement;
- Pro Forma Cash Flow Statement;
- Pro Forma Balance Sheet; and
- Ratio Analysis

7.2. Start-Up (Expansion) Cost Summary and Table

SOURCES OF EXPANSION CAPITAL	AMOUNT
Owner's Investment	$20,000.00
Bank Loan	$100,000.00
Total Expansion Capital	**$120,000.00**
EXPANSION EXPENSES	
Computers and Software	$15,000.00
Website and Supplies	$5,000.00
Legal and Consulting Expenses	$10,000.00
Purchase New Widget Manufacturing Equipment	$49,849.51
Miscellaneous Expansion Expenses	$2,500.00
Total Expansion Expenses	**$82,349.51**
WORKING CAPITAL BALANCE	**$37,650.49**

7.3. Break-Even Point Analysis

MWI must earn at least $1.2 million a year to break-even.

$300,000	÷	25%	=	$1,200,000

7.4. Pro Forma Sales Forecast

Product	Unit Sales FY-1	Unit Sales FY-2	Unit Sales FY-3	Total
Industrial Widgets	100,000	125,000 (+25%)	156,250 (+25%)	381,250
Deluxe Widgets	200,000	240,000 (+20%)	288,000 (+20%)	728,000
Standard Widgets	250,000	325,000 (+30%)	422,500 (+30%)	997,500
X-Widgets	----	----	32,500 (New)	32,500
Total	550,000	690,000 (≈25%)	900,000	2,140,000

Product	Selling Price	Revenue FY-1	Revenue FY-2	Revenue FY-3	Total Revenue FYs 1-3
Industrial Widgets	$8.50	$850,000	$1,062,500	$1,328,125	$3,240,625
Deluxe Widgets	$3.50	$700,000	$840,000	$1,008,000	$2,548,000
Standard Widgets	$1.80	$450,000	$585,000	$760,500	$1,795,000
X-Widgets	$59.25	$0	$0	$1,925,625	$1,925,625
Total		$2,000,000	$2,487,500	$5,022,250	$9,509,750

7.5. Pro Forma Income Statement

Widget Sales (Total Revenue)	$2,000,000	$2,487,500	$5,022,250
Cost of Goods Sold	– $400,000	– $500,000	– $1,250,000
Net Revenues	**$1,600,000**	**$1,987,500**	**$3,772,250**
Rents & Leases	$60,000	$72,000	$150,000
Telephones	$5,000	$6,000	$8,500
Utilities	$14,000	$17,000	$32,000
Payroll Expense	$1,148,000	$1,537,800	$1,994,080
Transportation & Shipping	$50,000	$70,000	$100,000
Business Insurance	$12,000	$15,000	$20,000
Computers	$12,000	$8,000	$48,000
Meals & Entertainment	$7,000	$8,500	$10,000
Travel	$14,000	$15,500	$18,000
Furniture, Fixtures & Equipment (FF&E)*	$56,000	$6,000	$18,000
Office Expense	$21,000	$32,000	$50,000
Office Supplies	$14,000	$15,000	$18,000
Widget Oil Expense	$2,000	$2,500	$3,000
Postage	$5,800	$7,400	$12,000
Total Expenses	**$1,420,800**	**$1,812,700**	**$2,481,580**
Profit / (Loss)	**$179,200**	**$174,800**	**$1,290,670**

7.6. Pro Forma Cash Flow Statement (Simplified)

Opening/Beginning Cash Balance	$275,000	$519,200	$369,000
Cash In from Operating Activities	$2,000,000	$2,487,500	$5,022,250
Cash In from Investing Activities	$50,000	($15,000)	$10,000
Cash In from Financing Activities	$100,000	$0	$0
Total Cash Available for Operations	**$2,425,000**	**$2,991,700**	**$5,401,250**
Cash Out from Operating Activities	$1,820,800	$2,312,700	$3,731,580
Cash Out from Investing Activities	$75,000	$300,000	$500,000
Cash Out from Financing Activities	$10,000	$10,000	$22,850
Total Cash Out	**$1,905,800**	**$2,622,700**	**$4,254,430**

7.7. Pro Forma Balance Sheet (FY-1)

Current Assets		Current Liabilities	
Cash	$300,000	Accounts Payable	$90,000
Savings	$50,000	Current Portion of Long-Term Debt	$10,000
Certificates of Deposit	$100,000	Short-Term Notes Payable	$50,000
Accounts Receivable	$175,000	-----	$0
Inventory	$125,000	-----	$0
Total Current Assets	**$750,000**	**Total Current Liabilities**	**$150,000**
Long-Term Assets		**Long-Term Liabilities**	
Machinery & Equipment	$500,000	Mortgages Payable	$510,000
Land & Buildings	$850,000	Loans Payable	$90,000
Total Long-Term Assets	**$1,350,000**	**Total Long-Term Liabilities**	**$600,000**
		Total Liabilities	**$750,000**
		Owner's Equity*	
		Paid-In Capital	$220,000
		Retained Earnings	$700,000
		Treasury Stock	$400,000
		Total Owner's Equity	**$1,350,000**
Total Assets	**$2,100,000**	**Total Liabilities & Owner's Equity**	**$2,100,000**

7.8. Ratio Analysis

CURRENT RATIO Current Assets ÷ Current Liabilities	$750,000 ÷ $150,000	5.0	MWI can pay off all current liabilities 5.0 times with current assets.
QUICK RATIO (Current Assets-Inventory) ÷ Current Liabilities	($750,000-$125,000) ÷ $150,000	4.17	MWI can pay off all current liabilities 4.17 times with quick assets and still have inventory left over.
GROSS MARGIN RATIO (Revenue-Cost of Goods Sold) ÷ Revenue	$2,000,000-$400,000) ÷ $2,000,000	80%	MWI has a high gross margin ratio so the company will have enough money (80%) to pay operating expenses.
PROFIT MARGIN RATIO Net Profit ÷ (Revenue-Cost of Goods Sold)	$179,000 ÷ ($2,000,000-$400,000)	11.9%	MWI converted 11.9% of sales into profits.
RETURN ON ASSETS Net Income ÷ Total Assets	$179,000 ÷ $2,100,000	8.5%	Every dollar that MWI invested in assets during the year produced $.085 of net income.
INVENTORY TURNOVER RATIO Cost of Goods Sold ÷ Average Inventory*	$400,000 ÷ [($0.00+$125,000)/2]	1.6	MWI sold its average inventory slightly more than 1½ times during the year.
DEBT RATIO Total Liabilities ÷ Total Assets	$750,000 ÷ $2,100,000	35.7%	MWI has over 3 times as many assets as liabilities, a relatively low debt ratio.
DEBT TO EQUITY RATIO Total Liabilities ÷ Total Equity	$750,000 ÷ $1,350,000	55.6%	MWI has slightly more than half as many liabilities than there is equity, meaning company assets are funded almost 2-to-1 by investors versus creditors.

Supporting Documents

MERIDIAN